WHAT HAPPENED ON THE *MARY CELESTE*

By the same author:

The First War Correspondent (William Howard Russell of *The Times*).
The Other Side of the Story.
Fact, Fake or Fable?
The Man Behind the Mask.
Myth and Mystery.
Famous Criminal Cases I-VII.
The Medical Murderer.
The Siege of Plevna (In U.S.A., *The Breakfast War*).
Tried By Their Peers.
Legend and Reality.
Tobias Furneaux, Circumnavigator.
The Two Stranglers of Rillington Place.
The World's Strangest Mysteries.
CRIME DOCUMENTARY. 1 : *Guenther Podola.*
2 : *Robert Hoolhouse.*
3 : *The Murder of Lord Erroll.*
4 : *Michael Davies.*
The Zulu War (Great Battles of History).
Courtroom U.S.A., I, II.
The Mystery of The Empty Tomb.
They Died by A Gun.
Massacre at Amritsar.

What Happened on the *Mary Celeste*

RUPERT FURNEAUX

MAX PARRISH · LONDON

Max Parrish & Co Ltd
6 Chandos Street
London W 1

Printed in Great Britain by
Waterlow & Sons Limited
Dunstable and London

CONTENTS

1

The drifting derelict

'Brig Ahoy'. The traditional call from one ship to another echoed across the stormy Atlantic wastes. 'Ahoy, Ahoy,' hailed the seamen standing in the bows of the *Dei Gratia.* No answering call came from the brig bowling past on the opposite tack. No helmsman stood at her wheel and her decks were silent and empty. She was sailing under short canvas and steering very wild and evidently in distress; every few minutes she yawed and fell off into the wind. Captain Morehouse had spotted her at 1 p.m. about 4 to 6 miles distant on the port bow. The strange ship was making about 1½ to 2 knots, heading westward, in the opposite direction to the *Dei Gratia.* The wind was north and the sea was running high. It had been blowing hard all morning with rain and squalls but was now abating. Something he observed through his spy-glass struck Captain Morehouse as strange. Whereas the brig was sailing on the port tack, her jib and fore-topmast staysail were set on the starboard tack.

Now, two hours later, Morehouse leant on the rail watching the brig careering along on her erratic course 300 yards away. 'Brace the yards and haul for that vessel,' he ordered Chief Mate Deveau, who had come on deck from his watch below. 'Look out for her name,' he shouted to his crew. All hands strained their eyes as the brig came plunging by. As she fell off in the wind, her stern came into view. 'It's the *Mary Celeste*', cried Helmsman John Johnson incredulously.

Astonished, Captain Morehouse echoed the name. The *Mary Celeste* was well known to him; her captain, Benjamin Briggs, his friend. Twenty-nine days before, they had dined together in New York. The *Mary Celeste*, an American-owned brig of 282 tons, bound for Genoa with a cargo of crude alcohol, sailed on 7 November, 1872, followed eight days later by the *Dei Gratia*, a Nova Scotian brigantine of 295 tons, bound for Gibraltar, where she was to await orders, with a cargo of petroleum.

Now the paths of the two ships had crossed at Latitude 38.20N by Longitude 17.15W, due east of the Azores, 591 miles from Gibraltar, on Wednesday 5 December, 1872, a date memorable in the history of the sea.

'Lower a boat and board her', Morehouse ordered Deveau.

*

The story of the drifting derelict, the *Mary Celeste*, is the Great Mystery of the Sea, the world's most famous enigma, an apparently insoluble problem, which has been discussed and argued about by three generations of amateur detectives. The story of the ship – undamaged, well found and fully provisioned, abandoned in mid-ocean – is so well known that it makes a stock question in television quiz programmes. 'Name the famous derelict' asks the inquisitor. 'The *Mary Celeste*' promptly replies the eighty-year-old pensioner, or teenage spiv, though usually referring to it *Marie Celeste*.

The American brig was found, the legend tells, with her sails set, her boats intact, a half-eaten breakfast on the cabin table, three cups of tea still warm to the touch, her cat calmly sleeping on a locker, no sign of damage or violence, and no one aboard. She was brought into Gibraltar by a prize-crew from the *Dei Gratia*. What happened to her captain, his wife, child and crew is a baffling mystery, for the solution of which countless theories have been offered.

Like hundreds of thousands, perhaps millions, of other people I became intrigued by the mystery. I had known of it from childhood. Sir Arthur Conan Doyle's famous, but fictional, solution, reprinted in a collection of his sea stories, set me thinking. Countless magazine and newspaper articles, each repeating or improving upon each other failed to satisfy me. I had investigated and written about such famous historical mysteries as the Man in the Iron Mask, the Prisoner in the Temple (Louis XVII), the Kensington Stone, the Money-Pit, the Strange Statues of Easter Island, and the murder problem of the Two Similar Stranglers of Rillington Place. Inevitably I turned to investigate the *Mary Celeste* – but where to start? That was the problem. The famous brig had been taken into Gibraltar, a British port, by a prize-crew from the *Dei Gratia*. There must therefore have been an inquiry. From the Registrar of the Supreme Court at Gibraltar I obtained the record of the evidence given to the Vice-Admiralty Court. From other sources I secured various official documents and reports. I turned up the files of contemporary newspapers and I traced many articles in British and American magazines. I have found three books dealing with the problem.

From these multitudinous sources I present The True Story of the *Mary Celeste*, 'untold', I claim, in the sense that the true facts and the story of the evolution of the legend have never before been collected and told completely in one book intended for popular reading. Two previous authors only have attempted to do so. Mr J. G. Lockhart, famous for his investigation of sea mysteries, wrote up the story in 1927, but his book *A Great Sea Mystery* is very short and it has been rendered obsolete by Mr Charles Edey Fay's *The Mary Celeste: The Odyssey of an Abandoned Ship*, whose detailed account was published in the United States only in a limited edition in 1942. Mr Fay, who drew on the files of the Atlantic Mutual Insurance Company of New York (which insured the ship and her freight) and on data collected privately in the United States, printed all the known facts, but he only briefly records the growth and evolution of the great myth, which is perhaps the most interesting part of the story, and he does not set out to examine in detail the many 'survivor stories' which have appeared from time to time. Thus, while paying tribute to Mr Fay's deep research work, and gratefully acknowledging the permission freely granted by his publishers, the Peabody Museum of Salem, Massachusetts, to utilise many of the documents there collected, I express the hope that my *What Happened on the Mary Celeste* will more readily satisfy the general reader, for whom Mr Fay's book was not intended. The third book, *The Great Mary Celeste Hoax*, by Laurence J. Keating, 1929, is dealt with later.

*

Oliver Deveau accompanied by two men from the *Dei Gratia*, Second Mate John Wright and Seaman John Johnson, rowed across the choppy sea to the *Mary Celeste*. On reaching her, Deveau and Wright clambered aboard leaving Johnson in the boat. What exactly Deveau and Wright found, or did not find, on the *Mary Celeste* was told by them at the Court of Inquiry at Gibraltar some weeks later, evidence with which we shall deal in due course. From what they then stated, we learn that when they hoisted themselves over the derelict's rail they came upon an eerie scene. No face or voice greeted them; no sound was to be heard save the creaking of the rigging, the slap of sails and the swish of the waves as the *Mary Celeste* careered on her headlong way. Unlashed and unmanned, the wheel turned and spun as the sea twisted the rudder. Two sails, the foresail and the upper fore-topsail, had been blown away and the lower fore-topsail hung by its four corners. The main staysail lay loose on the forward-house. All the other sails were furled. Some of the rigging was gone.

Cautiously Deveau and Wright stepped on to the deserted deck. Slowly and carefully they examined the ship from stem to stern. They searched the main cabin, looked down the forward hatch, which was open, peered into the forecastle and inspected the galley. No one was aboard, that was certain. Yet their quick survey showed that the *Mary Celeste* was perfectly sound, her hull, masts, rigging and sails in good condition, her cargo well stowed and intact, plenty of food and water aboard, and no sign of damage, disorder or confusion, and no reason why she might have been suddenly abandoned. Fit to 'go round the world' as Seaman Anderson was later to put it. A complete and baffling mystery.

True there was 3½ feet of water in the hold, and the cabin, forecastle and galley were a foot deep in water. But for a wooden ship of her size that was no more than normal leakage. The only sign of damage was that the binnacle had been knocked down, its glass broken, its compass destroyed. On the bunks in the forecastle lay the seamen's pipes, tobacco and clothes. In the cabin stood a harmonium, under the sofa lay a sewing machine. In the cabin was a clock which had stopped. On the bed was an impression of a body, one so small that it could have been made only by a child. The imprint of a tiny head was still visible on the pillow. The ship's crew and passengers had left in a great hurry.

On the cabin table the searchers found a chart showing the track of the vessel up to 24 November and a slate on which notes had been made for entry into the ship's log, showing that the last observation had been made at 8 a.m. on 25 November. The *Mary Celeste* had then been at Latitude 37.01N by Longitude 25.01W, 6 miles distant from the north-easterly point of the island of St Mary, the most easterly island of the Azores group. Now, ten days later, Deveau observed she was 378 miles to the north-eastwards, *still on her exact course to Gibraltar*, her first port of call. On the slate had been scribbled the words 'Fanny my dear wife. Frances M. R.' The writer had apparently been interrupted suddenly. The ship's navigational instruments and papers, with the exception of the log book, were missing, and the last entry, on 24 November, showed that the *Mary Celeste* had been then 110 miles westward of St Mary.

It was all very puzzling. A perplexing mystery. If the *Mary Celeste* had been abandoned or her crew had been lost in some way on 25 November, to which the entry on the slate seemed to point as the fatal day, how had she held her exact course for ten days unmanned and unsteered? And in that time she had sailed 378 miles. And sailed for ten days apparently with no one on board.

His cursory examination of the derelict finished, Deveau returned to the *Dei Gratia*, where he reported to Captain Morehouse. He asked to be allowed to take two men and sail the *Mary Celeste* to Gibraltar. Morehouse, while he did not wish to reject the opportunity of earning for himself, his crew and his owners a considerable award for salvage, was at first doubtful of the feasibility of the plan. To spare three men out of his small crew of eight might endanger the safety of his own vessel and cargo, and three men would be hard put to it to sail the derelict the near 600 miles to Gibraltar, a journey of unpredictable perils in mid-December. For a minute Morehouse strode up and down pondering the problem. Then he turned and told Deveau, whom he knew to be an experienced seaman and who had been Master of a brig, 'You can have your men'. In a moment all was bustle and activity. Collecting the food the Steward had prepared for their evening meal, a compass, a barometer, a watch and his own navigational instruments, Deveau stepped into the boat with Seamen Charles Lund and Augustus Anderson, who had agreed to go with him on the *Mary Celeste*. By 4 p.m. they were on board, and by 9 p.m. they had pumped her dry, set her sails and got her under way. But it took them two or three days to 'set her to rights' and 'make any headway'.

For several days the *Mary Celeste* and the *Dei Gratia* sailed towards Gibraltar in company, speaking to each other each night and morning.

2

To Gibraltar

The day before reaching Gibraltar, the *Mary Celeste* and the *Dei Gratia* became separated in a storm and the official record shows that the *Dei Gratia* entered the Straits on the evening of 12 December and the *Mary Celeste* early on the following morning, appropriately on Friday the Thirteenth.

The bringing into port of a derelict, yet staunch, vessel whose captain, Benjamin Briggs, was well known and respected in Gibraltar caused a sensation, and speculation became rife as to the reason why she might have been abandoned in mid-ocean, and what might have happened to her captain and crew ; excitement which was brought to fever pitch by the discovery in her cabin of a sword, the blade of which appeared to be blood-stained.

The *Mary Celeste* was taken into custody by T.J. Vecchio, the Master of the British Vice-Admiralty Court, a guard was placed on board and on 18 December the Court began the hearing of the claims of 'David Reed Morehouse, Master of the British brigantine *Dei Gratia* and for the owners, officers and crew of the said brigantine, claiming as salvors against the *Mary Celeste* and her cargo, proceeded against as derelict'. Sir James Cockrane, Knight and commissary of the Vice-Admiralty Court of Gibraltar presided. To these proceedings we will return later. The evidence taken was not then published and its details remained unknown to the world for seventy years. Sufficient is it to remark that testimony was given by the captain and crew of the *Dei Gratia*, and Captain James Winchester, part owner of the *Mary Celeste* who came from New York, supplied the names of the lost captain and crew. Captain Morehouse and the owners of the derelict were represented by advocates and Mr Solly Flood, the Queen's Proctor in Her Office of Admiralty and Attorney-General of Gibraltar, appeared for the Crown. These proceedings lasted on and off until 24 March, when the Court announced its verdict.

Meanwhile, the world was informed of the strange occurrence, the finding in mid-ocean of a staunch vessel fully provisioned and in a seaworthy condition apparently abandoned by her captain and crew. 'A marine tragedy,' as Mr Charles Edey Fay calls it, 'destined to become the most widely known of all the mysteries of the sea.'

On 16 and 17 December *Lloyd's List* recorded the arrival of the *Mary Celeste*, incorrectly described as an 'Austrian brig' at Gibraltar and stated that she had been taken into the possession of the Admiralty Court. The Liverpool *Daily Albion*, also noting her arrival, misnamed the ship that had found her as the '*Dia Gratio*'. The Liverpool *Mercury*, quoting the *Globe's* correspondent at Gibraltar, gave more details. It related that the *Mary Celeste* had been found abandoned under foremast staysail and jib; she had been pursuing her way for ten days without a soul on board; every document which could throw light on the mystery was gone; there was not the slightest clue to account for the desertion of the vessel and 'every conjecture is at fault'; the vessel had sustained no injury; a little phial of oil had been found standing by a sewing machine and a reel of cotton and a thimble 'not yet rolled off the table' in the cabin; the contents of the cabin indicated the one-time presence of a lady and child; a sword had been found and on it marks of blood; there were sharp cuts on the vessel's bulwarks. The whole thing was an absolute mystery. There was no trace of lady, child, captain or crew.

These newspaper reports from Gibraltar show, at least, that the 'Mystery of the *Mary Celeste*' was not a myth or romance conjured up by some fictional leg-puller, as was at one time suggested.

At Gibraltar the mystery ship was subjected to two surveys, the first taking five hours, on 23 December and 7 January, and her hull was examined by a diver. The surveyors' and diver's reports were published in the *Shipping Gazette* on 5 February 1873, and they are given in full in the Appendix.

The affidavit of Mr. John Austin, Surveyor of Shipping at Gibraltar, is of considerable length, and he states that the whole appearance of the vessel showed that she had never encountered any such violence as would have accounted for her abandonment. He found no wines or spirits on board. He made the most careful and minute examination through every part of the vessel to which he had access, and did not discover the slightest trace of there having been any explosion or any fire, or of anything calculated to create an alarm of an explosion or of fire. The vessel was thoroughly sound, staunch and strong, and not making water to any appreciable extent. He found on the bow, between two and three feet above the water line, on the port side, a long narrow strip of the edge of one of her outer planks cut away to the depths of about three-eighths of an inch, and about one inch and a quarter wide, for a length of about six or seven feet. The injury had been sustained very recently, and could not have been effected by weather, and was apparently done by a sharp instrument cutting continuously through the whole length of the injury. He found on the starboard bow, but a little further from the stem of the vessel, a precisely similar injury, but perhaps an eighth or a tenth of an inch wider, which in his opinion had been effected at the same time and by the same means. He adds that he was wholly unable to discover any reason whatever why the vessel was abandoned.

J. Ricardo Portunato, the diver, who had examined the hull of the vessel, states in his affidavit that the vessel did not exhibit any trace of damage or injury, or any other appearance that the vessel had been in collision or had struck upon any rock or shoal or had met with any other accident or casualty. The hull, keel, sternpost and rudder were in thoroughly good order and condition.

On 22 January, Mr Solly Flood reported to the Board of Trade in London, and his statement and opinions were printed by the *Gibraltar Guardian* on 14 February. To the Board of Trade he wrote:

> I have the honour to acquaint you, for the information of the Privy Council for Trade, that early on the morning of December 13, part of the crew of the British vessel *Dei Gratia*, bound from New York for Gibraltar for orders, brought into this port a brigantine, which they stated they had found on the 5th of that month in Latitude 38.20N, Longitude 17.15W,

at 3 p.m. sea time, totally abandoned and derelict, and which they supposed from the log to be the American brigantine *Mary Celeste*, bound from New York for Genoa. They stated that the wind being from the north, and the *Dei Gratia*, consequently, on the port tack, they met the derelict with her jib and foremast staysail set on the starboard tack. I caused the derelict to be arrested in the customary manner upon her arrival, whereupon the Master of the *Dei Gratia*, who had arrived on the evening of December 12th, made his claim for salvage. The second mate of the *Dei Gratia* and those of her crew who had boarded the derelict, were examined in support of the claim to salvage on the 20th and 21st ult. But the account which they gave of the soundness and good condition of the derelict was so extraordinary that I found it necessary to apply for a survey, which was held in my presence on the 23rd of the same month, and the result of which is embodied in the affidavit of Mr Ricardo Portunato, a diver, sworn on the 7th inst. of Mr John Austin, Master Surveyor of Shipping sworn on the 8th inst., and Mr T. J. Vecchio, sworn on the 9th inst. From that survey it appears that both bows of the derelict had been recently cut by a sharp instrument, but that she was thoroughly sound, staunch, strong, and in every way seaworthy and well found; that she was well provisioned, and that she had encountered no seriously heavy weather; and that no appearance of fire or of explosion, or of alarm of fire or explosion, or any other assignable cause for abandonment, was discoverable. A sword, however, was found, which appeared to me to exhibit traces of blood, and to have been wiped before being returned into its scabbard. My opinion in this respect having been corroborated by others, I proceeded on the 7th inst., to make, with the assistance of the Marshal of the Vice-Admiralty Court, a still more minute examination for marks of violence, and I had the honour of being accompanied and greatly assisted by Captain Fitzroy, R.N., H.M.S. *Minotaur*; Captain Adeane, R.N., H.M.S. *Agincourt*; Captain Dowell, C.B., R.N., H.M.S. *Hercules*; Captain Vansittart, R.N., H.M.S. *Sultan*; and by Colonel Laffan, R.E., all of whom agreed with me in opinion that the injury to the bows had been effected intentionally by a sharp instrument. On examining the starboard topgallant-rail, marks were discovered, apparently of blood, and a mark of a blow, apparently of a sharp axe. On descending through the fore hatch, a barrel, ostensibly of alcohol, appeared to have been tampered with. The vessel's Register, Manifest and Bills of Lading have not been found, neither has any sextant or chronometer been found. On the other hand, almost the whole personal effects of the Master, and, as I believe, of his wife and child, and of the crew, have been found in good order and condition. They are of considerable value. In the Captain's cabin were a harmonium in a rosewood case, books of music, and others mostly of a religious tendency; gold lockets and other trinkets, jewellery, and female attire of a superior description, were in the lady's boxes. The working chart and ship's log were also found on the arrest of the vessel. Both are complete up to noon of the 24th November. I transmit a copy of the last day's work; the deck or slate log is continued – copy of which is enclosed – up to 8 a.m. on the following day, at which hour the eastern point of St Mary's (Azores) bore S.S.W., distant six miles. She had therefore run considerably less number of knots since the previous noon than that entered in the slate, the longitude of St Mary's being 25.9W. Since then eight weeks have elapsed, and nothing whatever has been heard of the Master or crew, or of the unhappy lady and child. The ship's log, which was found on board, shows the last day's work of the ship up to noon on the 24th November, when the weather was sufficiently fine to enable an observation to be taken; the position then was by observation Latitude 36.56N, Longitude 27.20W. Entries on the log slate are carried up to 8 a.m. on the 25th, which is the last, and at which time she had passed from west to east to the north of the Island of St Mary's, the eastern point of which bore S.S.W. six miles distant. The distance of the longitude of the place where she was found from that last mentioned on the log is 1.18N., so that she must actually have held her course for ten days after November 25th, the wheel being loose all the time. My object is to move the Board of Trade to take such action as they may think fit to discover, if possible, the fate of the Master, his wife and child, and the crew of the derelict. My own theory or guess is, that the crew got at the alcohol, and in the fury of drunkenness murdered the Master, whose name was Briggs, his wife and child, and the chief mate; that they then damaged the bows of the vessel, with the view of giving it the appearance of having struck on rocks, or suffered a collision, so as to induce the Master of any vessel which might pick them up, if they saw her at some distance, to think her not worth attempting to save; and that they did, some time between the 25th November and the 5th December, escape on board some vessel bound for some North or South American port or the West Indies.

The day after penning this report, Mr Flood wrote further to the Board of Trade enclosing an extract from the log of the *Dei Gratia* as is necessary to show the position of that vessel on and from the 24th November to the day when she met the *Mary Celeste* on the 5th December from which it will appear that the wind during the whole of that time was more or less from the North, that she (i.e. the *Dei Gratia*) was during the whole of that time on the Port tack, and that consequently it seems incredible that the *Mary Celeste* should have run during the same period a distance of 7.54E at least on the starboard tack, upon which tack she was when met by the *Dei Gratia*.

Mr Flood went on to say:

> These circumstances seem to me to lead to the conclusion that – although no entry either in the Log or on the slate of the *Mary Celeste* later than 8 a.m. on 25 November is to be found, she had in fact not been abandoned till several days afterwards, and probably also that she was abandoned much further to the Eastward than the spot where she was found.

We have thus in the Admiralty Proctor's report to London the first theory of the cause of the abandonment of the *Mary Celeste*. Mr Solly Flood suspected that violence had occurred and murder had been done. The mutinous crew of murderers had escaped upon some other vessel, several days perhaps after the last log entry had been made, and they might be found and apprehended if diligent search was made. He would be thankful, he told the Board of Trade, for any information.

Mr Flood did not let the matter rest there. Although he had already caused two surveys of the vessel to be made, and he himself had made a detailed inspection, he now, on 27 January, ordered a further examination by Dr J. Patron who minutely inspected the *Mary Celeste*'s deck, topgallant rail, cabin floor, the sides of the berths, the mattresses, a piece of the vessel's timber which had been removed and lodged in the Proctor's office and several papers containing powderlike scrapings. He examined also the sword and its sheath which had been found in the cabin. He wrote his report on 30 January. It was not published and its contents remained unknown save to a few people in official circles, and we learn from a letter written by Consul Sprague on 4 April that it was not allowed to be opened 'even for the purpose of furnishing a copy to the Governor of the Fortress'. It was kept secret – apparently by Mr Flood himself – and it remained under seal in the possession of the Registrar of the Vice-Admiralty Court, Edward J. Baumgartner, for fourteen years, until, on 25 July 1887, at the instigation of the United States Department of State, it was opened in the presence of Proctor Solly Flood and Consul Sprague. It was found to confirm, says Sprague, his statement to the Department in 1873 regarding the mysterious sword 'that the result of it was considered to negative anything like blood existing therein', and he sent a certified copy of the report to Washington, where it exists still in the National Archives. In his letter to the Department, written on 1 February 1873, Sprague described the sword as 'of Italian make and bears a Cross of Savoy on the hilt.'

Why did Admiralty Proctor Solly Flood suppress the analyst's report? The only possible explanation for his secretiveness seems to be his disappointment that Dr Patron's report failed to support his theory of mutiny and murder, and he kept it hidden to save himself the embarrassment of admitting that his theory had little stronger basis than supposition. The key to this minor riddle may lie in Consul Sprague's estimate of Solly Flood as a man having a 'very vivid imagination' and in his statement to his superiors in Washington on 20 January, 1873, that 'the Queen's Proctor in the Vice-Admiralty Court of this city, who is also Attorney-General, seems to take a great interest in the case and rather entertains the apprehension of some foul-play having occurred.' In that communication Mr Sprague declared that 'the matter is wrapped up in mystery'. Mr Flood's opinion that 'the crew got at the alcohol and in the fury of drunkenness, murdered the Master, his wife and child, and the Chief Mate' seems to have been derived from the discovery, noticed by neither Mate Deveau or surveyor Austin, but made by the Admiralty Proctor himself, that a barrel of the ship's cargo 'ostensibly of alcohol appeared to have been tampered with'.

One broached barrel, a sword bearing what at first appeared to be blood stains but which were recognised to be only rust, and cuts on the *Mary Celeste's* bows were all that Mr Solly Flood had to go on. But mutiny and murder did seem to be a possible explanation.

Mr Sprague was far more cautious. Announcing the arrival in Gibraltar of Captain Winchester, he wrote to Washington on 20

January, 'In the meanwhile nothing is heard from the missing crew of the *Mary Celeste*, and in face of the apparent seaworthy condition of this vessel, it is difficult to account for her abandonment, particularly as her Master, who was well known, bore the highest character for seamanship and correctness: beside he had his wife and child with him and was part owner of the *Mary Celeste*.'

We may jump ahead at this stage to notice Mr Sprague's further reference to Captain Briggs, contained in a letter to Mr N.W. Bingham, U.S. Treasury Agent at Boston, written on 3 April, 'The missing Master I had known for many years and he always bore a good character as a Christian and an intelligent and active ship's master.'

Estimates of the missing Captain which were to remain unknown to the public for seventy years, in which time Captain Briggs's character was to be blackened by countless writers unaware of, and perhaps disinclined to discover, his good reputation and fine record as a seaman.

The *Dei Gratia* had been released on 23 December and she continued her voyage, being despatched to Genoa to unload her cargo, under the command of Mate Deveau. Captain Morehouse remained in Gibraltar, and on 15 January Captain Winchester arrived from New York to protect his vessel's interest and those of the New York underwriters. He entered a claim for the *Mary Celeste* and for the owners of the cargo at the Vice-Admiralty Court, and he gave evidence at its hearings of the claim for salvage. When he had completed his testimony he took himself off to Cadiz where he met Captain Harry O. Appleby, aged 22, who had gone to school with his daughter, in command of the brigantine *Daisy Boynton*.

To Appleby, Winchester explained his anxiety that the delay in releasing the *Mary Celeste* was running up expense and endangering her charter to load fruit at Messina for the return voyage to New York. Appleby, without seeking permission from his father, Captain Lemuel Appleby, the owner of his craft, lent the freight money he had earned to Winchester, the loan being secured on the hull of the *Mary Celeste*. Winchester, his immediate difficulties solved, went to Lisbon, from where he wrote to Consul Sprague on 6 February, announcing his intention to return to the United States. His sudden departure seems to have taken Sprague by surprise, for we find him writing to the Department of State on 12 February: 'he never announced his intention to the Court', and saying that Captain Winchester had given people in Gibraltar to understand that he was taking only a pleasure trip to Cadiz.

Captain Winchester wrote to Sprague from New York on 10 March enclosing a power of attorney showing that a man named Simpson Hart had acquired an interest in the *Mary Celeste* by loans made to Captain Briggs. Winchester went on to state that, on arriving home, he found his wife's condition of health had grown more serious and that his anxiety about her had caused his unexpected departure from Gibraltar. His presence there, he said, was accomplishing very little; he was under considerable expense and his business was suffering by his absence. The real pith of the letter came in its final paragraph. Winchester related that a gentleman came to him at Gibraltar and told him 'that after the Judge and the Attorney-General had used up every other pretence to cause delay and expense, they were going to arrest him for hiring the crew to make away with the officers'. 'This idea,' wrote Captain Winchester, 'was very ridiculous, but from what you and everybody else in Gibraltar has told me about the Attorney-General, I did not know but he might do it, as they seemed to do just as they liked. When I left Gibraltar I expected to go back, but after talking with the Consul at Cadiz, I decided to come home. All the other legalised documents you now have.'

A further development occurred on 5 February when the United States cruiser *Plymouth* called at Gibraltar and, at the request of Consul Sprague, its commanding officer, Captain R. W. Shufeldt, made an inspection of the derelict which was exciting so much curiosity. His report, which was dispatched to Washington by Sprague on the following day, formed the subject of an article published in the Liverpool *Mercury* on 15 March, and reprinted on the 29th by the New York *Nautical Gazette*, which expressed the fears of the State Department that murder had been committed by a drunken crew who had either perished at sea or escaped on some other vessel. An opinion not shared apparently by Captain Shufeldt about whose examination the *Mercury* told its readers:

We have been specially favoured with a copy of the final report made by Captain Shufeldt of the United States ship *Plymouth* after a special visit paid by him to the derelict *Mary Celeste*. Captain Shufeldt, like everyone else who has *examined the ship*, is of the opinion that she was abandoned *in a moment of panic* by the master and the crew. He considers that she may have strained in a gale, and, for the time, creaked so much as to seriously alarm the master, and it is probable that, at the time, another vessel coming in sight induced him – as his wife and child were on board – to abandon his ship thus hastily. Should the surmise be correct, the time which must have elapsed before he and his crew are again heard of, must depend upon the distance of the port to which the rescuing vessel happens to be bound. Captain Shufeldt altogether rejects the idea of a mutiny, because there is no evidence at all of violence about the decks or in the cabin, and with regard to the damage about the bows of the ship, he considers that it merely amounts to splinters in the bending of the planks, which were afterwards forced off by the action of the sea, and not in any way betokening any intention of wilfully damaging the vessel. The *Mary Celeste* is confessed on all hands to be, at the present moment, staunch and seaworthy, and Captain Shufeldt maintains that the master and crew will be either heard of some day or, if not, they have perished in the boat for which they abandoned their own ship. For the present the mystery remains unsolved, but it is satisfactory to note that the opinion of a *practical man*, such as Captain Shufeldt is, and the analysis made by Doctor Paton (i.e. Patron) of this city (Gibraltar), of the alleged bloodstains coincide in refuting the theory of violence. The possible fate of those who were on board the *Mary Celeste* is sad enough, without the addition of mutiny and bloodshed. It will be observed that the opinion of Captain Shufeldt is in direct contradiction to that expressed by the surveyors here.

Here, then, we have the second theory of the cause of the *Mary Celeste's* abandonment. The captain and crew had left their ship in a moment of panic. They might have perished or they might still be heard of. Captain Shufeldt's theory was in direct contradiction to that held by Proctor Flood who was supported in his belief that mutiny and murder had been done by the report of the Surveyor of Shipping that the damage to the bows had been caused intentionally.

Following the order of events, we note that on 31 January Justice

Cockrane, on being petitioned for the release of the *Mary Celeste*, so that she could continue her voyage and land her cargo at Genoa, sharply criticized the departure from Gibraltar of Mate Deveau, calling it 'most reprehensible'. He said it was very strange that the captain of the *Dei Gratia* 'who knows little or nothing to help the investigation' should have remained in Gibraltar while the first mate and crew who had boarded the derelict should have been allowed to go away. In consequence of this stricture, Deveau was ordered to leave his vessel at Genoa and return to Gibraltar where he was recalled to give further testimony before the Court of Inquiry. That Sir James Cockrane shared the Admiralty Proctor's suspicions of high foul play is suggested by the words by which he rejected the claim for the *Mary Celeste's* release. Replying to the petition he emphasised 'there are certain matters which have been brought to my notice respecting this vessel, my opinion about which I have already very decidedly expressed, and which make it desirable, and even necessary, that further investigation should take place before the release of the vessel can be sanctioned, or before she can quit this port.'

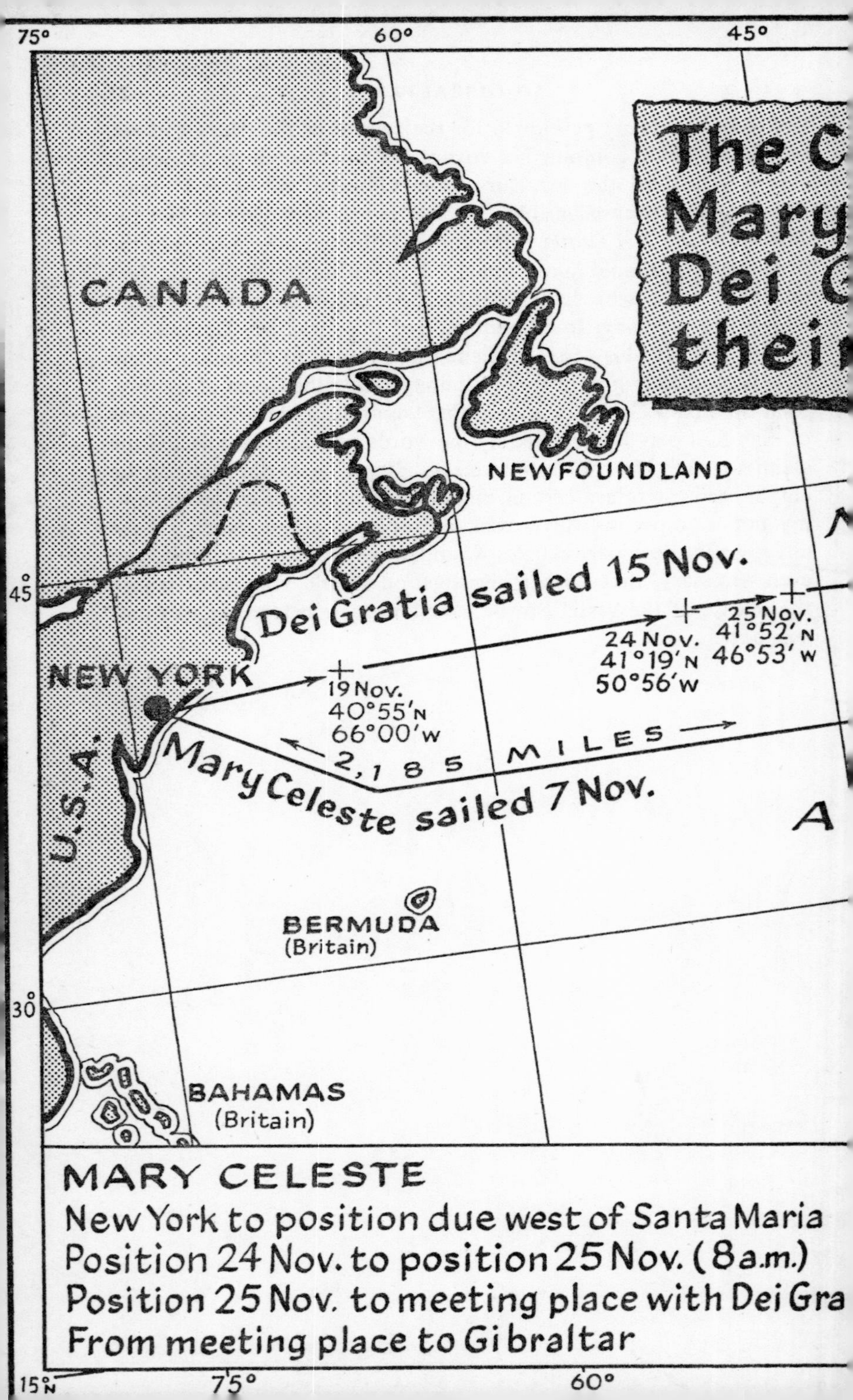

75°
60°
45°
The C
Mary
Dei G
their
CANADA
NEWFOUNDLAND
45°
Dei Gratia sailed 15 Nov.
24 Nov.
41°19'N
50°56'W
25 Nov.
41°52'N
46°53'W
NEW YORK
19 Nov.
40°55'N
66°00'W
2,185 MILES
Mary Celeste sailed 7 Nov.
U.S.A.
A
BERMUDA
(Britain)
30°
BAHAMAS
(Britain)
MARY CELESTE
New York to position due west of Santa Maria
Position 24 Nov. to position 25 Nov. (8 a.m.)
Position 25 Nov. to meeting place with Dei Gra
From meeting place to Gibraltar
15°N
75°
60°

30° 15°

ses of the
este and
cia from
gs, 1872

BRITISH
ISLES

FRANCE

45°

30 Nov.
41° 15′N
30°15′W

Dec. (5th.)
38° 20′N
17° 50′W

PORTUGAL

SPAIN

GIBRALTAR
12/13 Dec.

RTH

25 Nov.
37°01′N
25°01′W

AZORES
(Portugal)

Santa Maria

Cape
Spartel

CEUTA

24 Nov.
36°56′N
27°20′W

MADEIRA
(Portugal)

30°

ANTIC

CANARY
ISLANDS
(Spain)

N

AFRICA

CEAN

CAPE
VERDE
ISLANDS
(Portugal)

15°

miles
miles
miles
miles

30° 15°

3

The salvage award

Newspapers published in cities in which interest in maritime affairs was paramount kept their readers informed of news of the drifting derelict, the Liverpool *Mercury* stating under the heading of 'MYSTERIOUS OCCURRENCE AT SEA' that not the slightest clue had been found to account for the desertion of the vessel by her crew and the *Boston Post* attributing her abandonment to her being seized by pirates who 'after murdering the Captain, his wife, child and officers' abandoned the vessel near the Azores, to which islands they had probably escaped and where they would be found if diligent search was made. The crew, the *Post* stated, consisted 'mostly o f foreigners' and it suggested 'that some of the men probably obtained access to the cargo and were thus stimulated to the desperate deed.' The general opinion at Gibraltar, the *Post* reported, was that there had been foul play on board 'as spots of blood on the blade of a sword, in the cabin, and on the rails, with a sharp cut on the wood indicate force or violence having been used, but how or by whom is the question'.

Another red-herring, which was to lead to incalculable repercussions, was started by the *New York Sun* which alleged on 12 March, 1873, that the *Mary Celeste* had been irregularly registered as an American vessel, part of a scheme to defraud insurance companies, a suggestion which was labelled as an atrocious falsehood by Captain Winchester.

The State Department at Washington was brought into the

inquiry, and it was supplied with the information collected at Gibraltar by the British Minister who stated in a letter written on 11 March, 1873:

> You will perceive that the inquiries which have been instituted into this matter tend to arouse grave suspicions that the Master of the Vessel in question, together with his wife and child, were murdered by the crew who would seem subsequently to have abandoned the Vessel, and are supposed either to have perished at Sea, or to have been picked up by a passing vessel. It is under these circumstances that I have been instructed to communicate the inclosed documents to you, in order that, if the Government of the United States should think it expedient, investigations may be instituted with a view to obtaining some clue to the cause of the derelict vessel having been abandoned.

The world hunt for the derelict's missing captain and crew was put into operation on 24 March by the United States Treasury Department which issued the following instructions to all customs officers, a circular which the reader will perceive contained three inaccuracies: the date on which the *Mary Celeste* was found, her longitude at the time, and the method by which she was brought into Gibraltar.

> CIRCULAR RELATIVE TO THE BRIGANTINE MARY CELESTE FOUND DERELICT AT SEA.
>
> You are requested to furnish this department with any information which you may be able to obtain affording a clue to the discovery of the facts concerning a vessel found on 13th December last, in Latitude 38° 20N, and Longitude 17° 51W, derelict at sea and which was towed into the harbour at Gibraltar by the British vessel *Dei Gratia* and there libelled by the salvors. From the log of the abandoned vessel, she is supposed to be the American brigantine *Mary Celeste* bound from New York for Genoa, and it is supposed that she sailed from New York and that her master's name was Briggs. The circumstances of the case tend to rouse grave suspicion that the master and his wife and perhaps their child and the chief mate were murdered. Many other details concerning the matter are in possession of the department and, if necessary, they will be furnished upon application.
>
> (signed) William A. Richardson,
> *Secretary of the Treasury.*

This official circular bruited about the world Mr Solly Flood's theory of 'foul play', which, as we have seen, was based on nothing stronger than suspicion but which we may agree appeared at that time to be the only feasible explanation of what was apparently inexplicable.

In Gibraltar the *Mary Celeste* was restored to her owners on 25 February and, after a detention of 87 days, she sailed to complete her voyage and discharge her cargo at Genoa on 10 March under the command of Captain George W. Blatchford of Wrentham, Massachusetts, who had been brought from New York for that purpose by the ship's owners, with a new crew. She arrived at Genoa on 21 March as was reported by the New York *Maritime Register* on 9 April, 1873.

From a letter written from Genoa on 26 April by U.S. Consul O.M. Spencer to Consul Sprague we learn that 1701 barrels of alcohol, of which 9 were empty, were landed, and that the cargo came out in excellent condition 'so much so that the consignee, who wished to relinquish it in favor of the underwriters, could find no excuse for doing so.'

In Genoa, reported the New York *Journal of Commerce* on 13 May, the *Mary Celeste* was hove down, her bottom surveyed and 'found in perfect order'.

We may remark here that the *Dei Gratia* reached New York on her homeward voyage on 19 June, and the *Mary Celeste* docked at Boston on 1 September, sailing on for New York which she reached on 19 September.

On 24 March the Vice-Admiralty Court gave judgement in the case of the derelict *Mary Celeste*, awarding the sum of £1,700 ($8,300) to the master and crew of the Nova Scotia brigantine *Dei Gratia* for the salvage services rendered by them; the costs of the suit to be paid out of the property salved. The *Gibraltar Chronicle* reported that the *Mary Celeste* was valued at $5,708 and her cargo at $36,943, totalling $42,673, 'so that the award may be set down as one-fifth of the total value'.

To this brief announcement the *Gibraltar Chronicle and Commercial Intelligencer* added:

The judge thought it right to express the disapprobation of the

> court as to the conduct of the Master of the *Dei Gratia* in allowing the first mate, Oliver Deveau to do away with the vessel which had rendered necessary the analysis of the supposed spots or stains of blood found on the deck of the *Mary Celeste* and on the sword, and his Lordship also decided that the costs of the analysis should be charged against the amount awarded to the salvor.

The enquiry disclosed that the *Mary Celeste* herself was insured by the Atlantic Mutual Insurance Company of New York for $14,000, and her cargo, which was shipped by Messrs. Meissner and Ackerman of New York at a charge of $3,400, was insured in London for £6,522 3s. 0d.

The proportionate share of the cargo owners, about 80% of the total, was therefore, by Mr Charles Edey Fay's analysis, about $6,640, leaving a balance of about $1,660 to be found by the American underwriters insuring the respective interests of hull and freight.

One-fifth of the total value of ship and cargo was a small award, and Mr Fay records that in an address on Maritime Insurance given at Yale University on 22 February, 1904, which was published in the *Yale Alumni Weekly* on 2 March, Mr Anton Adolph Raven, former President of the Atlantic Mutual Insurance Company, called it a 'moderate compensation, being only about 18% on an aggregate value of $47,000 for vessel and cargo', adding 'it is not unusual, when derelicts – i.e. abandoned vessels – are picked up at sea, for a salvage award of more than twice that percentage to be made to the salvors.'

'Evidence is not wanting,' says Mr Fay, 'that there was some dissatisfaction on the part of the owners of the *Dei Gratia* and of Oliver Deveau, first mate, in connection with their respective shares of the award.'

Captain Morehouse and his men had reason to be dissatisfied. The reward for their exertions was a poor one. Had the British Vice-Admiralty Court reason to be suspicious of their claim? That is a question to which we shall return.

With the unsatisfactory outcome of the Inquiry, which had failed after three months to find any reason for the abandonment of the *Mary Celeste*, the personal effects of her missing captain and crew were returned to New York by Consul Sprague who sent also the harmonium found in the cabin and the now famous sword for delivery to Mr James C. Briggs, the brother of the derelict's missing captain. Meanwhile Mr Sprague had received a query from the German government regarding the missing seamen who were of that nationality, and to this he replied on 4 April, stating that he regretted to report he was still without tidings, and saying that 'the general opinion is that no violence took place on board, as no signs were found to that effect'. After stating the names believed to be those of the missing crew, he promised the German official that he would not fail to inform him of any further information which might come to light relating to 'this mysterious affair'. The correspondence was re-opened in 1885.

The hope that the missing captain, his wife and child, and crew of the ill-fated *Mary Celeste* might turn up somewhere continued to prevail for several months. Meanwhile, the mystery had been heightened rather than lessened by the events at Gibraltar. The *Mary Celeste* had sailed from New York well found, well provisioned and staunch, commanded by an experienced master with an adequate crew of eight. In all ten people had been on board. When found, she was in a seaworthy condition, and she had apparently been abandoned in a great hurry. Those were the salient facts which created the mystery in the first place. The *Mary Celeste* was no abandoned hulk, with which the North Atlantic was strewn in that stormy winter of 1872–3, as the shipping columns of contemporary newspapers show. There seemed to be only three possible explanations for the mystery. Her captain and crew had abandoned the vessel of their own free will in a moment of panic, as Captain Shufedlt surmised. Or the captain, his wife and child and the mate had been the victims of foul play – as the imaginative Mr Flood theorised. Or Captain Winchester had 'hired the crew to do away with the officers', i.e., an insurance fiddle, as the words of that gentleman's informant in Gibraltar seemed to suggest.

It was all very puzzling and strange. No wonder the mystery of the drifting derelict caught the imagination of the world right from the start.

Not surprisingly, extreme excitement was caused in shipping circles in May, 1873, when the following news report was published by the Liverpool *Daily Albion* on 16 May:

> A SAD STORY OF THE SEA – A telegram from Madrid says:— Some fishermen at Baudas, in Asturias, have found two rafts, the first with a corpse lashed to it, and an Agrican (? American) flag flying, and the second raft with five decomposed bodies. It is not known to what vessel they belonged.

Were these bodies the final clue to the mystery of the *Mary Celeste?* Perhaps they were those of six members of her crew, but they could equally well have belonged to one of the hundred or so sailing vessels reported missing that winter from New England ports. By a strange coincidence, Captain Oliver Briggs, brother of the missing master of the *Mary Celeste*, was lost in his own ship, the *Julia A. Hallock*, in the Bay of Biscay. Dr Oliver Cobb, a cousin of the Briggs family, has disclosed that the two brothers had arranged to meet in the Spring of 1873 at Barcelona to load fruit for the homeward voyage to New York. Two days out from Vigo, in Northern Spain, the *Julia A. Hallock*, which was carrying a cargo of fine coal, sprang a leak. The ship's pumps became clogged and unworkable and she filled with water and capsized, all on board drowning except Second-Mate Perry, who, after drifting for five days on a piece of wreckage, was picked up by a Spanish vessel. This disaster, says Dr Cobb, must have preceded by only a short time the one that befell Captain Benjamin Briggs, and it would have remained just as impenetrable a mystery but for the rescue of Perry.

Without reliable information, hope for the *Mary Celeste's* captain and crew faded, and the mystery of their fate became intensified. Why had they, or some of them, abandoned their staunch vessel in such a hurry? No answer could be derived from the *Mary Celeste* herself, and these goading questions threw the field wide open to speculation. Nine years were to elapse before the first 'true solution' to the mystery was offered.

4

Conan Doyle takes the helm

The ill-fated *Mary Celeste*, and the mystery surrounding the disappearance of all on board quickly faded out of the news, becoming submerged by the famous controversy relating to the audacious claim of the Wapping butcher, Arthur Orton, to be the long-lost Roger Tichborne, the heir to great estates in England, which provided our grandfathers with ten years of heated argument, to the exclusion of almost all else. Public interest in the drifting derelict had been whetted but hardly excited. A few facts had been published, two theories had been advanced. Either her crew got drunk and murdered their officers, or Captain, officers and crew deserted their staunch and sound vessel in sudden panic. There was suspicion, conjecture, nothing more. The true facts relating to her discovery in mid-Atlantic remained unknown, locked away in the files of the Supreme Court at Gibraltar. The *Mary Celeste* became forgotten, the fate of her crew a passing nine-days' wonder, just another mystery of the sea which provided many mysteries.

But one man did not forget the story he had heard in his childhood. In 1883 he was a young doctor struggling to establish a practice in Portsmouth, England. To augment his income, he wrote stories for boys' magazines for which he was paid £4 each. Searching his mind for something more ambitious and rewarding, he recalled the mystery of the drifting derelict which had made such a stir ten years before. Solving mysteries came easily to the young doctor who four years later made his name by the publication of his first Sherlock

Holmes story, *The Study in Scarlet.*

Sir Arthur Conan Doyle's solution to the mystery forms an immense landmark in the evolution of the *Mary Celeste* myth. His reconstruction of the disaster that befel her people was published, anonymously according to its rule, by the *Cornhill Magazine*, in January 1884 as 'J. Habakuk Jephson's Statement' which purported to tell the story of a passenger, the only survivor of the voyage. It was reprinted in 1890 in a collection of the author's sea stories entitled *The Captain of the Polestar*, after Conan Doyle had become world famous as the creator of the Great Deductive Reasoner, the Baker Street detective whom many people then believed to be a real person. Why not therefore 'J. Habakuk Jephson'?

As well as telling Jephson's story, Conan Doyle related a number of 'facts' about the *Mary Celeste* and her voyage. Unfortunately for truth, but luckily for our amusement' the true facts about the '*Marie*' *Celeste*, as Conan Doyle misnamed her, were as unknown to him as they were then to the world. He felt required to give his story some semblance of truth and he did so by quoting a non-existent newspaper, the *Gibraltar Gazette*, which, according to him reported in its issue of 4 January (as the curious could find for themselves, he remarked) that when she was found the derelict's boats were intact and slung upon their davits. How then had her people left her?

By this mis-statement of fact, Conan Doyle turned a minor puzzle into a mystery of truly mammoth proportions: one which posed a conundrum which was to set half the world arguing; for the *Mary Celeste*, with her boats intact, presented a problem which could be explained only by extravagant theories.

Where Conan Doyle obtained the idea that the *Mary Celeste's* boats were intact is beyond our knowledge, for in his *Memories and Adventures*, published in 1924, he is exasperatingly reticent about 'J. Habakuk Jephson's Statement'. Conan Doyle, of course, may have invented the presence of the boat or boats, or he may have inferred that they were intact from Mr Solly Flood's misleading remark, in his Report to the Board of Trade, which suggested that the missing crew had escaped on board some other vessel.

Conan Doyle told his story with a wealth of detail, giving it just those little touches which make the tall story ring true. The circumstances of the discovery of the vessel had excided considerable comment at the time and had aroused a curiosity which had never been satisfied, he reminded his readers. The '*Marie*' *Celeste*, he revealed, carried three passengers, one of them J. Habakuk Jephson 'the well-known Brooklyn specialist on consumption', who was a distinguished advocate for the Abolition of Slavery, and whose pamphlet 'Where is Thy Brother?' had exercised a strong influence on public opinion in America. (These biographical details authenticated the story which was to come.) In his Statement, which is written in the first person, J. Habakuk Jephson declares his intention to tell all he knows of the ill-fated voyage, which he sees as a duty he owes society.

Continuing with the narrative, Dr Jephson explains why he has not proclaimed himself before, and why he has suffered so many conjectures and surmises to pass unchallenged. If by revealing them the ends of justice could have been served, 'I should have unhesitatingly have done so', he says. But when he tried to do so to an English official he was met with such offensive incredulity that he determined never again to expose himself to the chance of such an indignity. Even his relatives listened to his statement with 'an indulgent smile', and only his son's solicitations changed his resolution to let the matter sink into oblivion.

Conan Doyle's story was of course pure fiction. And a very good story he made of it. Another passenger, a sinister half-caste from New Orleans named Septiminus Goring, who has contrived to replace two of the crew with men of his own, quietly murders the '*Marie*' *Celeste's* officers and the captain's family, who disappear utterly and entirely. Captain 'Tibbs' goes mad and shoots himself. Dr Jephson is saved from a similar fate owing to his possession of a black stone, shaped like a human ear, an object of veneration by the negroes. Goring interferes with the ship's navigational instruments, and Dr Jephson awakes one morning to find the ship is lying off the coast of Africa where, Septiminus Goring tells him, he intends to found a Black Empire. Dr Jephson's talisman saves him again and, after the '*Marie*' *Celeste* has been cast adrift, he is placed in a boat which is picked up five days later by a steamer which carries him to Liverpool. He concludes his Statement with these solemn words:

From the day on which I found myself once more in the bosom

of my family I have said little of what I have undergone. The subject is still an intensely painful one to me, and the little which I have dropped has been discredited. I now put the facts before the public as they occurred, careless how far they may be believed, and simply writing them down because my lung is growing weaker, and I feel the responsibility of holding my peace longer. I make no vague statement. Turn to your map of Africa. There above Cape Blanco where the land trends away north and south from the westernmost point of the continent, there it is that Septiminus Goring still reigns over his dark subjects, unless retribution has overtaken him; and there, where the long green ridges run swiftly in to roar and hiss upon the hot yellow sand, it is there that Harton (another passenger) lies with Hyson (the mate) and the other poor fellows who were done to death in the *Marie Celeste*.

A story for which Conan Doyle was paid the princely sum of £30.

Both Consul Sprague and Proctor Solly Flood read 'J. Habakuk Jephson's Statement'. Sprague sent a copy of the *Cornhill Magazine* to the State Department in Washington with the comment that it seemed to be 'replete with romance of a very unlikely or exaggerated nature'. Nonetheless, he urged the American authorities to try to trace the author of 'this extraordinary composition', receiving the reply that as the mystery was 'in no wise explained' by the Statement, the Department 'did not deem it essential to propose any particular enquiries into the antecedents of the writer of the article in question'.

Mr Solly Flood, however, seems to have been excited by the story, which he described in a letter to Sprague as 'professing to have been written by an eye-witness', and he took the opportunity to tell the American Consul that he was in correspondence with officials in Germany, which tended to confirm his belief that survivors of the vessel's abandonment were still hiding in that country; an opinion which Sprague found unsupported by the Chief of the Parish of Utersum auf Fohr, which, we shall learn, was the home of some members of the *Mary Celeste's* crew. This rumour, stated the Chief of the Parish in February, 1885, 'appears to have been inspired by misleading statements now beginning to appear in the newspapers', a remark which confirms that Conan Doyle's story had started the Great Myth rolling, the snowball of myth and mystery which was soon to overrun the world.

On 3 January, 1885, while the world was pondering the increasingly famous mystery of her abandonment in 1872, the *Mary Celeste* was wrecked on Roskell's Reef, off the coast of Haiti in the West Indies, and her timbers were left to rot.

5

The great myth gathers momentum

The disastrous end of the ill-fated brig, following so closely upon the publication of 'J. Habakuk Jephson's Statement', revived interest in the mystery surrounding the *Mary Celeste's* abandonment in 1872, and it gave a new impetus to speculation about the fate of Captain Briggs, his wife, child and crew – who, if the boats were intact, must obviously have been spirited away from their vessel. Speculation became directed to the means by which they could have left her, which resulted in the advancement of a number of theories and in further misrepresentation of facts. The existence by 1905 of a fully-fledged myth, as solid as the Rock of Gibraltar itself and as impervious to assault, indicates that in the twenty years following upon the publication of Conan Doyle's fictional solution, the Great Myth grew in leaps and bounds, so much so that a commentator writing as early as January, 1886, found himself able to tell his American readers that there had already been much speculation as to the cause of the vessel's abandonment, which was held, he said, to be a mystery 'the solving of which would make anyone famous'.

These twenty years in which the myth grew and exaggeration was piled on each new improvement can best be described as a sort of 'tunnel' period, like that in which an underground stream flows and grows in strength, occasionally bubbling to the surface. Only here and there do we catch a glimpse of the great debate, but it is clear that many people were talking about the *Mary Celeste*, for by 1905 the well known 'credo' was fully established, and most, if not all, the famous theories had been evolved. From one mouth to another grew the story of the staunch and sound vessel under full sail, with a half-eaten breakfast on the cabin table, three cups of tea still warm to the touch, the captain's watch still ticking, the cat sleeping peacefully on a locker, the seamen's washing hanging out to dry, the galley fire burning brightly, the chicken boiling in the pot, the boats swinging from their davits, and not a soul on board.

Here and there we can trace the origin of some of these improvements to the story and they need to be disposed of before we can consider the true facts as disclosed by the testimony given in Gibraltar in 1872 by the men of the *Dei Gratia*.

Captain Coffin, for instance, who wrote up the mystery in the *New York World* on 24 January, 1886, was guilty of originating, or perhaps only of repeating, a further inaccuracy which in time was to provide another commentator with a 'fact' to bolster his particular theory. Coffin, while he stated truthfully that the *Mary Celeste's* long boat was missing, said that the forehatch was found lying *bottom* up on the deck which suggested it might have been blown off by an explosion. There was very little mystery about the vessel's abandonment, Captain Coffin told his readers, and he quoted the theory put forward a few days earlier to a reporter of the *World* by Captain Winchester, the erstwhile principal owner of the *Mary Celeste*.

While it is not yet opportune for us to consider Captain Winchester's explanation of the mystery (which, as we shall see, was adopted and presented in 1925 and 1940 by Dr Oliver Cobb, Benjamin Briggs's cousin), we need to note, in order to do Captain Coffin justice, that he described it in 1886 as 'the true explanation of the cause of the abandonment'. It will not be out of place, however, for us to notice Captain Winchester's comments about Benjamin Briggs whom he called a 'fine man' and 'as smart a ship-master as ever trod a deck', and his opinion that the vessel's mate, Richardson, was a man of 'excellent character'. The steward, he said, was a white man who was respected by all who knew him, and the crew 'were all Germans and were the nicest set of men I ever saw on board a ship'; first-hand character references in respect of the missing men which the myth-makers and theorisers preferred to ignore.

Captain Coffin provided his readers with a plausible explanation of the apparently strange fact that the derelict had kept her exact course for ten days, but he perpetrated several further inaccuracies, one of which provided an author in 1929, as we shall see, with a means of suggesting there had been a criminal conspiracy between the crews of the *Mary Celeste* and the *Dei Gratia.*

The great avalanche of inaccuracies and theories was still to come; Clark Russell, the novelist, appears to have been responsible for the unconsumed meal and the brightly burning galley fire. He presented his ingenious solution for the derelict's abandonment in a fictional story entitled 'The Mystery of the Ocean Star', which was clearly stimulated by the mystery of the *Mary Celeste.* This appeared in *Longman's Magazine* on 10 August, 1887, and was reprinted in a collection of his maritime sketches under that name in 1888, published in London. In it he tells how the steamship *Guide*, coming out of a fog, encounters the *Ocean Star* drifting about with her sails in some disorder. The steamer's mate, on boarding the bark, finds the galley fire burning brightly and recently tended, for the coal is still spitting out gas flames, and a fowl boiling in a saucepan on the stove. The ship's boat is missing and the last entry in the log is dated ten days back, indicating the absence of the master, yet the fresh galley fire shows the recent presence of someone on board.

A salvage crew is put aboard and the vessels part company. Next day, the *Guide* picks up some of the missing crew and the mystery is partially cleared up. The *Ocean Star* had suffered a series of misfortunes; the captain was found dead in his bed; the first mate died of fever; two seamen were killed in accidents; the second mate while examining the rudder fell overboard; the crew lowered a boat and went to his rescue, leaving one man on board; those in the boat got lost in a fog and, the wind freshening, the bark ran away. When the *Guide* was sighted, the remaining seaman sprang on the rail to signal her, tripped, fell overboard and was drowned.

As a novelist's reconstruction the story was a good one, though it is wildly unlikely that such a chapter of accidents could have befallen one ship, which, according to the author, sailed from Hull for Rio in 1877. But, like Conan Doyle before him, Clark Russell established mis-statements of fact which were in time to take on the semblance of 'Gospel Truth'.

Some time during this 'tunnel' period, it was suggested that the

Captain and crew had deserted their vessel from fear of a gigantic iceberg which appeared to be bearing down on them, a theory rendered unlikely by the position of the *Mary Celeste* – far to the south of the limits of arctic ice even during the spring melting period. References found later show that the theory that the cook poisoned all on board and fell into the sea himself while disposing of his victims' bodies also came into being at this time, as probably did the 'pirate' theory. Another theory which must have been put forward about this time suggested that the people of the *Mary Celeste* had been stricken with plague and had fallen overboard in their agony.

To account for the disappearance of the crew, someone hit upon the brilliant idea that the *Mary Celeste* must have been taken by Barbary or Riff pirates and her crew carried off to North Africa as slaves. At first sight this seems a plausible solution to the mystery, and as it was repeated as late as 1933, it is advisable to dispose of it now. The Algerine and Salle corsairs, who preyed upon shipping for centuries, and even raided the southern coasts of Britain, were destroyed in 1816, due to a remarkable example of international co-operation. Between 1801 and 1813 the young United States navy bombarded and burnt the ports of Algiers, Tunis and Tripoli, and in 1816 a joint British and Dutch expedition blew Algiers apart. Pirates were therefore few and far between in 1872.

Another widely held theory, one that bounced up quite often, is that the abandonment of the vessel and the disappearance of her people had something to do with the weather, a solution to the puzzle which appeared to be borne out by the terrible gales of that winter which, in the words of the *Annual Register*, 'abounded in violence and frequency' and led to 'the disastrous record of wrecks and casualties at sea'. Great gales swept the Atlantic at the end of November, and the gale that hit London on 8 December is described as the most severe for centuries and recalled memories of the winds which accompanied Cromwell's death in 1658. November, 1872, was marked in many parts of the world by wonderful displays of meteors and on the 27th of that month the earth is said to have been swept by the *disjecta membra* of Biela's lost comet. These natural phenomena were employed to explain the mystery, on the assumption that they had caused Captain Briggs to order the abandonment of his ship. But the evidence proves that the *Mary Celeste* had suffered no damage from storms, and the record of her log, and that of the *Dei Gratia*, indicate that neither ship encountered any exceptionally bad weather during their voyage across the Atlantic.

Following the progress of the Great *Mary Celeste* Myth, we find that by 1902 it had gathered so much momentum that an enterprising newspaper sought the views of the widow of the missing mate, and on 9 March, Mrs Fanny Richardson stated certain new 'facts', and gave her own theory in the *Brooklyn Daily Eagle*. Her late husband, she said, though a qualified captain, had shipped under Captain Briggs, taking the position of mate temporarily while awaiting the command of another vessel then fitting out. Briggs, who was accompanied by his wife and two year-old daughter, Richardson, and William Head, the steward were the only Americans on board, the crew being composed of foreigners; Italians, Turks and Portuguese. These were said to have been 'as bad a looking lot as ever swabbed a deck' – the newspaper commenting, 'and this fact has always tended to shed a more lurid light around the mystery'. Captains Briggs and Morehouse are stated to have been acquainted and to have met and talked about their respective voyages, parting with mutual good wishes, before the *Dei Gratia* sailed several days *ahead* of the *Mary Celeste*.

'I always believed and always will believe that my husband, Captain Briggs, Mrs Briggs, her baby and the cook were murdered by the crew', Mrs Richardson told the *Eagle's* reporter. Her husband, she stated, had a presentiment of evil before he sailed, and he appeared to her in a dream on the night of 24 November, the date on which she believed the catastrophe occurred. Her brother-in-law, Captain Lyman Richardson, on the other hand, thought, she said, that those on board the *Mary Celeste* had been done away with by the crew of the *Dei Gratia*, and she said that he had sailed the seas for several years in an assumed character for the purpose of ascertaining if there was anything in his theory.

Apart from the theories she made public, Mrs Richardson's interview did provide investigators with some useful information. She stated that the ship's boat was missing from its davits, and that the cradle on the foreward hatch intended to carry an additional boat had been smashed during the loading of the cargo, and Captain Briggs proposed to get a new long-boat on his arrival at Genoa.

She recorded, too, the discovery of the words scratched on the ship's slate, 'Fanny, my dear wife'; evidently the opening words of a letter, hurriedly abandoned, by the mate to his wife, whose name was Frances. She went on to state that when Mate 'Devon' of the *Dei Gratia*, as she calls Deveau, raised the hatch cover to examine the cargo, he found the head of a barrel of alcohol apparently blown off by an explosion. This, he believed, had so scared those on board that, fearing the balance of the cargo would explode, all hands had at once deserted the ship; a reflection, as we shall see, of the theory put forward by Captain Winchester as early as 1886.

She did not agree that fear of explosion had caused the abandonment of the vessel, Mrs Richardson said. She thought it far more likely that the crew broke the barrel open, drank the contents, murdered the four Americans and got away in the after boat. That was the real solution to the mystery, she maintained. The *Brooklyn Daily Eagle* did not find itself able to endorse fully Mrs Richardson's theory, and it commented that the solution to the mystery 'will probably never be learned until the sea gives up its dead.'

Mrs Richardson's theory did not satisfy Mr J. L. Hornibrook, a British author, whom we find writing on 'The Case of the "*Marie*" *Celeste*; an Ocean Mystery' in *Chambers' Journal* in September, 1904. His story is so representative of the fictions which were repeatedly told of the finding of the *Mary Celeste* that it deserves more than passing notice. Besides that, he had a new and startling theory to offer, but one which, as we shall learn, he had abandoned by 1933 when he had a quite different solution to offer. In 1904, Mr Hornibrook wrote:

> On a certain morning, back in the sixties, the Spanish authorities near the Straits of Gibraltar noticed a vessel in the offing which speedily attracted special attention. She was a brig, with all sails set, and at first sight appeared to be heading direct for the Straits, as though to enter the Mediterranean.
>
> A few minutes' scrutiny, however, revealed the fact that there was something wrong on board – something strange and inexplicable. Though the sea was calm and the weather fine, the brig did not hold straight on her course for two minutes together. She wobbled about and veered round with every changing puff of wind as if bereft of a guiding hand and left to stagger blindly onwards of her own accord.

A boat was quickly manned and put off to the vessel, for it was seen by this time that she was not under control. As the men drew near they hailed her more than once, but no answer came back to them from the brig. They now perceived that the wheel was deserted; nor was a single soul observable on deck. Not without a certain misgiving, and an instinctive dread of some appalling sight which might meet their gaze, they boarded the strange vessel. The reality, though it differed essentially from what they had expected, was scarcely less startling, The brig was absolutely devoid of life. The entire crew, from captain to cabin-boy had disappeared – vanished! A minute examination of the vessel revealed a truly extraordinary and astounding state of affairs. There was not a single boat missing. They were all in their proper places, slung on the davits and stowed on deck in the usual manner. Further than that, not a rope or stay, not a sail or spar, was injured. Everything, from truck to keel, was as sound as the day the vessel had sailed. More astonishing still, the captain's watch was ticking on a nail above his berth, and on the cabin table was found the remains of a half-consumed dinner, apparently as fresh as when it came from the cook's galley. The same thing was noticeable in the men's quarters, and looked as though the entire crew had been interrupted or startled in the midst of their meal. And that was all. Below, as on deck, there was deadness and silence – a ghostly, mysterious silence, all the more appalling by reason of its inexplicable nature.

The brig was navigated into Gibraltar, and there the American consul came on board, for, as was seen by the name of her port on the stern, she hailed from Boston. He, in turn, proceeded to make a minute and searching inspection, overhauling the vessel from stem to stern, and noting every detail. The only fresh discovery was something which looked like the slash of an axe or cutlass on the bulwark forward; but this, in itself, was calculated to throw little light upon the mystery.

Let us now turn to the commencement of this remarkable voyage, which ended in such a mysterious and unaccountable manner. The *Marie Celeste* set sail from Boston under the most favourable auspices, and certainly there was nothing either in her complement or otherwise to warrant the assumption that the voyage would result in tragedy of any kind. She was an ordinary trading brig, bound for the Mediterranean ports with a general cargo of merchandise. Her crew consisted of seventeen hands, composed chiefly of Americans, Danes and Norwegians. In addition, there was the captain, his wife, and their little daughter – twenty souls, all told.

Nothing, so far as is known, occurred during the voyage

across the Atlantic other than the ordinary routine of life on board a vessel of this class. Not until the brig came within sight of the Spanish coast, or nearly so, did the catastrophe occur; and then it must have been of a sudden, overwhelming and appalling character. The half-consumed dinners pointed to the fact that the crew were below at the time, undisturbed by any thought of approaching calamity.

From that day to this the fate of these twenty souls has remained an inscrutable and insoluble mystery. Nothing was ever heard of them, though the most searching inquiries were made on both sides of the Atlantic. Every sailors' home was notified by the American authorities, in case a stray seaman from the brig might turn up there. No intelligence ever came to hand. Not even a wave-washed bottle containing a message was cast up by the sea, nor a single body.

Of the various theories advanced in explanation of this singular ocean mystery, many may be dismissed as wholly untenable. Piracy may be put on one side, for piracy was as unknown in the Atlantic in the sixties as it is at the present day. Besides, if pirates had boarded the vessel and murdered the crew they must have left traces of their deadly work; not to mention the fact that they would scarcely have taken their departure without looting her from stem to stern.

It is equally impossible to suppose that the crew deserted the brig in a sudden panic, caused by the fear of her sinking, for not a single boat was missing. Nor was their disappearance due to a storm which swept every soul overboard. Storms leave abundant traces of havoc among sails and rigging.

The idea that every human being on board suddenly went mad and voluntarily cast themselves into the sea is altogether too far-fetched. It has been suggested, on the other hand, that one of the crew may have been attacked by homicidal mania, and murdered his fellows. But if so, where were the bodies? Even supposing that he had succeeded in his desperate attempt – one against seventeen – threw the bodies overboard, and finally plunged into the sea himself, traces of the tragedy would have been noticeable everywhere.

One truly startling and surprising theory would seem to cover the entire facts. American scientists were consulted at the time as to the possibility of the catastrophe being due to the attack of some terrible monster of the deep. They scouted the idea. We have now, however, a much more intimate and extensive knowledge of these sea-monsters; and the theory alluded to attributes the disappearance of the crew to the agency of a huge octopus or devil-fish. The scene might be depicted somewhat as follows:

> There is a man stationed at the wheel. He is alone on deck, all the others having gone below to their mid-day meal. Suddenly a huge octopus rises from the deep, and rearing one of its terrible arms aloft encircles the helmsman. His yells bring every soul on board rushing on deck. One by one they are caught by the waving, wriggling arms and swept overboard. Then, freighted with its living load, the monster slowly sinks into the deep again, leaving no traces of its attacks.
>
> It may be pointed out, in support of this theory, that the mark of a slash on the bulwark of the vessel would look as if some member of the crew had seized an axe and attempted to chop off one of the threatening arms. If, however, the theory be not accepted, it must be left to the reader's imagination to furnish a better one.

Thus, according to Mr Hornibrook, the *Mary Celeste* was not found by the *Dei Gratia* but by the Spanish authorities, a mis-statement of fact which was to provide Mr Keating in 1929 with a suspicious chain of events which enabled him to present perhaps the most startling 'solution' ever advanced about the derelict.

Mr Hornibrook's other so-called facts, we note, include the ship's boats slung on their davits, and the remains of a half-consumed dinner, which was to become, when some bright observer recalled that the last entry on the log-slate had been made at 8.0 a.m., a half-eaten breakfast. The *Mary Celeste* sails from Boston, not New York, her crew consists of 17 hands, and there are 20 souls on board. The catastrophe occurs near the Spanish coast, 600 miles from where the derelict was actually found. His account is noteworthy also for the statement that the mythical watch was still ticking. So do great myths grow by exaggeration. Some one learned that a clock had been found in the vessel's cabin; it becomes the missing captain's watch, and to emphasise the recent desertion of the vessel, it is stated to have been still ticking. It is surprising only that some investigator has not discovered that it had just been wound!

Above all, Mr Hornibrook had introduced the startling theory of the giant octopus, apparently the only possible means by which the disappearance of the vessel's people could be explained – once Conan Doyle had established the 'fact' that the boats were intact.

Apart from this brief excursion into the Atlantic by a British author to solve the mystery which was now gaining international fame, most of the contributions of this period appeared in American newspapers and periodicals.

The *New York Evening Post* revived 'THE STRANGE CASE OF THE *MARY CELESTE*' in its Saturday Supplement on 15 October, 1904, headlining it as 'A MYSTERY OF THE DEEP WHICH HAS NEVER BEEN SOLVED', and giving its story the lurid sub-heading:

> AN AMERICAN SHIP FOUND ABANDONED ON THE HIGH SEAS UNDER FULL SAIL – VARIOUS THEORIES AS TO WHY SHE WAS DESERTED – NOTHING EVER LEARNED AS TO THE FATE OF HER CAPTAIN AND CREW. SUBSEQUENT CAREER OF THE VESSEL.

Its reporter, Allan Kelly, did a service to truth by dismissing as sailors' stories, the brightly-burning galley fire, the untasted food, scarcely cold, set out ready to serve, the ticking clock and the missing boat. These, he observed, were 'fanciful touches, useful perhaps to a writer of fiction, but not to be included in a statement of fact.' Captain Winchester, he said, had refused to accept the mutiny theory, for the mate was of excellent character, and the crew were quiet, decent Germans, and in such a ship's company mutiny was highly improbable.'

Allan Kelly also refuted the theory, which must have been going the rounds – arising from the loss of the *Mary Celeste* in 1885 which resulted in her captain, Gilman C. Parker, being tried for deliberately wrecking his vessel – that Captain Briggs might have intended to wreck his ship on one of the reefs of the Azores. It was reported, Allan Kelly said, that Briggs headed her for the reef; pretended that she would not mind her helm, and ordered all hands into the boat; that after the crew left her, the wind hauled and so changed her course that she ran safely past the reef and scudded away. The obvious objection to the theory, observes Mr Kelly, was that Captain Briggs would not have taken his wife and child on the voyage had he intended to lose his ship; that he would not have risked their lives in a small boat very far from the islands, and that, had he tried the trick near the islands, he would almost certainly have reached shore.

Re-assessing the facts known about the sails, Mr Kelly points out that, just before abandonment, the vessel was evidently running before a strong breeze and she had been rounded to, he suggested, in order to enable the crew to launch the long boat. The fore-hatch, he said, was lying bottom upward on the deck, thus repeating an already established inaccuracy. Concluding his reasoned review of the mystery, Allan Kelly advanced the theory that the menace of sudden disaster had caused the captain to order the crew to leave the vessel.

The year 1905 saw two brief mentions of the mystery, both in American periodicals, the first in *McClure's Magazine* in May, when P.T.MacGrath, who was described as the author of *The Peril of the Iceberg* and *The Ocean Graveyard*, contributed an article entitled 'The Terror of the Sea', in which he dealt with the menace of derelicts to shipping. Amongst other well known instances of ships wrecked or abandoned, he cited, as the most extraordinary of all, the *Marie Celeste* which he described as a 'more fantastic creation, apparently, than novelist ever wrote'. This vessel, he stated incorrectly, left New York in 1887, with thirteen people on board. Two weeks later she was sighted by a British bark and found to have no sign of life on board. An exhaustive search proved her to be 'as silent as the tomb, as deserted as a pesthouse'. Everything was in its place, even the boats at the davits. Yet thirteen people had disappeared as if spirited away by some supernatural agency, and the author concluded by stating, 'and from that day to this the mystery has never been unravelled though the United States Government spared no effort to solve it'.

The second reference to the *Mary Celeste* in 1905 is found in the September issue of *Munsey's Magazine*, in an article by John R. Spears called 'Mysteries of the Sea'. In a short note, the author set out most of the true facts, mis-stating only that a stained and naked cutlass was found on the floor of the cabin and on the table a small bottle of medicine which had not been upset, showing that the vessel had drifted over smooth seas. Why she was abandoned, and what became of her crew, are questions that have never been answered, Mr Spears announced.

Some time in 1904 or 1905 a Liverpool newspaper printed the story of a SKELETON'S TALE IN A BOTTLE which was reprinted by the London *Daily Express* on 7 December, 1913, with the subtitle THE FATE OF THE MARIE CELESTE. This 'solution' of the mystery, stated the *Express*, was supplied by a Mr R. E. Greenhough, who said that in 1904 or 1905 he was serving as an apprentice on the barque *Ardorinha*, bound from Swansea, South Wales, to Chile, and who stated he was sent with a boat's crew to collect sand from the tiny islands of St Paul's Rocks. There they found a skeleton propped up in the shade of a rock, and by it a bottle stuffed with soiled and faded paper. The writing, which was in German, stated:

> I am dying. My ship struck these rocks at dawn three days ago. She sank immediately. Only I of all her crew reached the shore alive. There is no water; I am dying of thirst.
>
> It has been a voyage of disaster . . . killed in the engine room. Three deaths in two days. Then came the poison on the seventh day out.
>
> Chronometer had run down. In my agony I forgot to wind. Only one on ship. It was the final catastrophe. Ship helpless. Too weak to get steam on boilers. And so for three days we lay.
>
> Knew we must ask assistance to take us to Gibraltar for crew. That was ruin. Ship not insured. If English found cargo it was prison and confiscation.
>
> Managed to get steam to give steerage way. I headed for Lisbon. Early morning sighted small brig becalmed. Mate said 'Take her crew'. It was the Devil's voice.
>
> Went aboard. Captain asked why we came. His wife and child were with him. It was hard. It would have been easy without the woman. But the mate got behind the captain, he and two others, and threw him. His wife fainted. Then we pointed pistols. Crew went into boat quietly. One man shot. He fell into the sea . . .
>
> We left no one on board. The brig was called *Marie Celeste*. Would to God I had never seen her. Then the child would be yet alive. I cannot forget the child.

Commenting on this message so strangely brought to light after more than thirty years, the *Express* pointed out that one of the strangest features of the mystery was that no attempt had been made to launch the *Mary Celeste's* boats. It observed that no mention of the steamer's name was made in the sailor's story and it quotes Mr Greenhough as saying, 'There is little doubt that she was engaged in a trade requiring secrecy.'

Turning from sheer melodrama to real cloak and dagger stuff, we are told, by Mr Lockhart, that in 1909 the *Gibraltar Chronicle* received a message in cipher accompanied by a letter from 'one Ramon Alvarado of Cincinnati, Ohio, dated August 10th, 1909, which informed the newspaper that the key to the mystery of the *Mary Celeste* was to be found in the cipher message. This is apparently in some form of shorthand, but so far no one has been successful in decoding it. It is perhaps permissible to add that no one is recommended to waste very much time on it.'

My enquiry addressed to that newspaper brought a reply from its Editor, dated 4 July 1962, who informed me, 'I am sorry to say that so far as I know the cipher message and letter of 1909 referring to the *Mary Celeste* was not published, nor do I think it now exists.'

Finally, before concluding this chapter dealing with the evolution and development of the Myth, it is necessary to record that the *Nautical Gazette*, an American magazine, published on 24 December, 1913, an interview with Mr Winchester Noyes, a grandson of Captain James Winchester, who had died in the previous January. This repeated the *Mary Celeste's* principal owner's theory why her captain and crew deserted her, an explanation of her abandonment to which we shall return in a later chapter.

6

The *Strand* invites solutions

The year 1913 marks the moment when the Mystery of the *Mary Celeste* became world famous.

In the forty years which had elapsed since the discovery of the drifting derelict, the mystery of her abandonment and the fate of her master, his family and crew, had been discussed in a number of locally circulating newspapers and magazines in Britain and in the United States. The *Strand Magazine*, a London periodical of international reputation, now carried it to a wider public by reprinting an article which appeared in April 1913 in the *Nautical Magazine*, a journal circulating amongst merchant navy officers.

'What is the greatest mystery of the sea?' asked its author, who signed himself 'J.S.C.' Every deep-water sailor would answer – 'the *Marie Celeste*', he declared. Why she was abandoned and what became of her crew were riddles which had been discussed for thirty-eight years without result. There was ample room for imagination, he suggested.

In his résumé of the 'known' facts, J.S.C. introduced an entirely new element into the mystery, one which was to reappear frequently in the story – a German tramp steamer which was circling the derelict as the *Dei Gratia* came up. Captain 'Boyce' of the *Dei Gratia*, (the *Mary Celeste's* master is, we note, named 'Griggs') boards the derelict with the mate, the uncanny silence making their flesh creep. Theories of mutiny, piracy, storm, famine or sickness, are dismissed by the bewildered officers, and the possibility that the vessel's people have been devoured by a sea-serpent is considered, but cast aside. Whatever was the cause of abandonment, it is evident that those on board left in an awful hurry, without a stitch of clothing, in the middle of their breakfast and, of course, without their boats.

There is no clue to her desertion. It is a hard nautical knot, one which the reader must unravel for himself, states 'J.S.C.', and he makes a number of statements which show that, by 1913, the legend had undergone even further improvements. The sewing-machine found in the cabin was in actual use, a child's pinafore was in the process of being mended. The woman aboard had stopped sewing in the middle of stitching a sleeve, remarks the mate. 'No, she didn't', replies the captain. 'She stopped to get her breakfast', pointing to the cabin table which gives the appearance of four persons having risen from a half-eaten meal, now no longer designated merely as 'breakfast', but minutely described as consisting of oatmeal, coffee, bacon and eggs. The child had almost finished her porridge; the captain had just sliced his boiled egg in half. At the moment he had broken the shell, he left the cabin, never to return. At the woman's place stands a bottle of cough mixture; her last act had been to remove the cork and not a drop of medicine had spilled from the opened bottle. The forecastle, too, showed that the crew were about to sit down to their breakfast when they precipitantly 'went over the side'.

The last entry in the log had been made only forty-odd hours before the *Dei Gratia* found the derelict, and it had been made at 7 a.m. on the morning of 7 September, 1872. Clearly all hands had left in a great hurry on the spur of the moment. In the mate's room lay a paper containing a sum in addition; of the three columns only the first had been added, a statement of 'fact' which Mr Keating was to find useful in 1929. The sailors hadn't even stopped to take their pipes or tobacco, which led 'J.S.C.' to enquire 'Was the thing so terrible that it had induced sailors to not stop even for their smokes?' How could they have left except in the boats of another ship? he asked, adding the curdling thought, 'What message of mortal terror could that other vessel have brought to necessitate the immediate desertion of a staunch ship?'

The missing mate of the '*Marie*' *Celeste*, thus following Conan

Doyle's mis-spelling of her name, was named 'Henry Bilson', asserts 'J.S.C.', thereby providing another writer with the audacious claim that none of the crew named at Gibraltar in 1873 by Captain Winchester ever sailed on the *Mary Celeste*. The *Mary Celeste*, after her return to the United States in 1873, was black-listed by sailors as a 'hoodoo' ship, claims 'J.S.C.', and he says she was then engaged in shady enterprises, manned by men willing to disregard the hoodoo for the sake of the promised gain. When one captain sought a crew, the first sailor backed away with a horror-stricken look, a second turned on his heel and quickly walked away. Only the offer of double wages and extra rations could induce men to serve on the ship with the bad name.

The *Nautical Magazine's* story was as mythical as the sources from which 'J.S.C.' drew his information. About the only correct fact he stated was the date on which the *Mary Celeste* was found. The tonnage of the *Mary Celeste* was increased to '500 tons', those on board were given the magical and sinister number of thirteen, and the Briggs children were stated to be seven and twelve years of age. The dates given were inconsistent, inasmuch as the last entry in the *Mary Celeste's* Log is said to have been at 7 a.m. on 2 September, 1872, 'forty hours before' she was found on 5 December, and elsewhere it is stated that 'the Log shows nothing since leaving Sandy Hook', the point of departure from New York harbour, and early in September the *Mary Celeste* is still loading at her wharf in New York. The distance from the spot where the *Mary Celeste* was found to Gibraltar is incorrectly stated as being 300 miles. The sea is described as being as calm as a millpond and when the captain and mate of the *Dei Gratia* (Captain Morehouse did not leave his ship) board her it is called 'calm'.

The *Strand Magazine*, which reprinted these absurdities, invited four famous novelists to solve the mystery. 'Whether our readers think that any of them completely solve the mystery, or whether they themselves can suggest something more plausible, now remains to be seen', announced the *Strand*.

The first of the invited 'detectives' was Barry Pain, an author famous for his humour. His solution to the mystery was fear. He felt that the idea that all the thirteen persons on board went mad simultaneously and jumped overboard asked too much of coincidence. They must have left in a boat belonging to another vessel, therefore the boat that came alongside 'contained in it the source of the terror which led to the abandonment of the brig'. What was the nature of that terror? asked Barry Pain. There was no sign of a struggle, no bloodshed 'but an unarmed man who has a loaded revolver pointed at him does not struggle', he darkly observed. He does what he is told by the man holding the gun.

Barry Pain's solution was straightforward. A ship engaged in a nefarious enterprise loses her crew from fever. There are not enough hands to work the ship. Her captain sights the *Mary Celeste*, boards her and carries off her crew. What was their fate on the mysterious vessel? They may have died of fever too, suggests the author, though he envisaged the possibility that some may have survived and kept silent, because they had been compelled to engage in dishonest work.

The next novelist was short and brief. Morley Roberts, who was born in 1857 and died in 1942, had at least some knowledge of the sea; for he sailed 'before the mast' in his youth and lived in the South Seas, writing many sea-stories based on his experiences. He wrote:

> 'I have thought of the "*Marie*" *Celeste* at intervals for thirty years, and have never yet made the wildest shot at a solution. The data are insufficient to draw any conclusion from. If we knew the history of everyone on board, something might be suggested. It is, of course easy enough to cook up a fictional hypothesis, but that is simply supplying the very facts we can't get at. The explanation is almost certainly simpler than the problem, but more complex. I have sometimes thought it was a 'put-up' job, arranged by the captain for some reason, and his plan went wrong. Perhaps there was finance at the bottom of it. The fact that on analysis the notion of blood on the sword and woodwork was negatived makes what looks like a clue as vain as everything else.'

Mr. Roberts' sea-experiences evidently inclined him to realism!

Mr. Horace Annesley Vachell inclined to a more fantastic solution. Born in 1861 and living to the age of ninety-four, Mr Vachell wrote many novels, some of them 'mysteries', which were made famous by his character of 'Quinney'. He explained the mystery by suggesting an unforseen phenomenon which caused every soul on board to leap over the side and perish. His phenomenon? A submarine explosion which released a noxious gas, affecting the *Mary Celeste's* people instantly. Each became raving mad and plunged into the sea, which swallowed them and their secret. The whole ship's company perished. He made the conjecture at hazard, emphasized Mr Vachell.

Finally, Mr Arthur Morrison, in the words of the Editor of the *Strand* 'cast his solution in the form of a little story'. Mr Morrison, an English novelist and dramatist, an authority on the Far East and an early writer of detective fiction (his detective, 'Martin Hewitt', has been called 'the first detective of conspicuous note to follow in the footsteps of Sherlock Holmes') was born in 1863 and died in 1945. The crew of the *Mary Celeste* included a homicidal maniac, he suggested. This man whom he named 'Holy Joe', was a religious crank. One by one he seizes and throws overboard each member of the crew, the captain, his wife and child. The maniac dances alone on the empty deck. Finally he jumps overboard, clutching the ship's chronometer in his arms. 'The *Marie Celeste* dipped and yawed, took the wind again and drifted off on the calm Atlantic', believed Mr Morrison.

While none of these solutions did anything to solve the mystery, they show the tremendous interest it aroused in 1913, and how completely baffling it was to a generation which had been brought up to believe, on the impeccable authority of the creator of Sherlock Holmes, that none of the vessel's boats were missing.

The *Nautical Magazine*, not to be outdone by the *Strand* which had stolen its fire, in its December, 1913, issue published a still further solution to the mystery, introducing 'love' on board the *Mary Celeste*. Its correspondent, Mr William Bernstein, an elderly marine-engineer, wrote suggesting that the mate fell desperately in love with the captain's wife, and he was at all hazards determined to win his prize. By a remarkable coincidence another vessel hove in sight. She was desperately in need of men. Aided by the love-sick mate her captain impressed the *Mary Celeste's* crew. What happened to the strange vessel carrying the derelict's people? She foundered with all hands, declared Mr Bernstein, which was not a very original solution to the mystery which all England was now discussing, and half the world was pondering.

Fictional as clearly were these solutions to the now famous Mystery, they were to have a startling repercussion.

7

The yarn of Abel Fosdyk

The world was treated now to the first 'survivor' story which purported to supply the true solution to the problem about which everyone was talking. It came to the *Strand Magazine*, which published it in November 1913, with a covering letter. A 'sensational development' had taken place with regard to this remarkable mystery of which a full account had appeared in the July issue, announced the *Strand*. Before introducing the 'extraordinary document' which had come into its possession, the *Strand* recapitulated in a few words the story 'of what has become universally known as the greatest mystery of the sea'. The article published in July, stated the *Strand*, 'has brought to light – in addition to some hundreds of more or less ingenious guesses – an account so vivid and alive, yet so simple and yet so unlikely to be thought of, that one seems to hear the ring of truth on every page'. It had been sent to them by Mr A. Howard Linford, the headmaster of Peterborough Lodge – Hampstead's largest preparatory school. The *Strand* stated:

> Mr Linford is well known in the scholastic world as a man who has fought hard for the better teaching of mathematics and English to the young as being the essentials of a scientific training. He has met his just reward by the successes of his pupils in the public schools. When King Edward VII opened the New Speech Room at Rugby it was to a former pupil of Mr Linford's that His Majesty handed the gold medal for English. The Shakespeare prizes last year and this year at Harrow and

Westminster went to other old boys, as did also both gold medals for mathematics. The mathematical scholarships gained by his boys are probably more numerous than those of any other preparatory school in England, and he numbers amongst his pupils the sons of some of the most distinguished scientists of England and France.

'With these few preliminary remarks we leave the letter and document to speak for themselves', stated the *Strand*, and we will follow the same course. Mr Linford wrote to the Editor:

Sir – A friend has brought to my notice your article on the '*Marie Celeste*'. When I read it the name struck a familiar chord, but I was some days before I could remember under what circumstances I had heard it. At last, however, I recalled an old servant, Abel Fosdyk, committing to my charge, on his death-bed, a quantity of papers contained in three boxes; amongst these he told me would be found the account of (the) *Mary Celeste*. I suppose he said 'the', but I had at the time no notion of what Mary Celeste meant, and imagined it was a woman. I paid but little heed, and merely sent the boxes away to a safe keeping, not anticipating they would ever be opened again. Before commenting on the matter I would like to emphasize the fact that I do not vouch for the truth of anything narrated. No word on the subject was ever mentioned by the writer to me. But the fact that for thirty years he kept not only a diary but also a set of shrewd observations on all that passed, and wrote much and well without our knowing anything of what he was doing, shows him to have been a man of exceptional reticence and self-control.

As for the document, I would rather let it speak for itself; but at the same time I must confess I have been greatly impressed by the following facts: A *brig* called '*Marie Celeste*' sailing under Captain *Griggs* is under discussion. I find an account of a *brigantine* named '*Mary Celeste*', sailing under a Captain *Briggs*. By your courtesy I have now seen the official report, and find in every instance the papers in my possession are correct. Further, the official papers mention a peculiar damage to the bows and two square cuts on the outside. This, I think, has never till now been made public, yet here again the papers I send you enter most minutely into the alteration of the bows. Finally, I find, on inquiry, that the autumn of 1872 was famous for its extraordinary storms in the Atlantic, so much so that a leading article in *The Times* likens it to the period of storms so well known to have prevailed at Cromwell's death. One can easily imagine a captain, working day and night in such conditions, going gradually out of his mind.

Of course, minute errors will always creep in when relating facts a long time after their occurrence. It is evident to me these facts were written down nearly twenty years after they happened, and no one knows better than myself how easily dates may be forgotten or the sequence of events confused.

I now leave the MS in your hands.

A. HOWARD LINFORD M.A.
(Magdalen College,
Oxford).

Peterborough Lodge,
Finchley Road, N.W.

To this the *Strand* added the comment, 'One word is necessary with regard to the illustrations. The son of this gentleman – then a boy at Harrow – having some artistic gift, was in the habit of making sketches under the old man's directions, but without knowing for what purpose he wanted them. These have been placed at our disposal and have been made use of in illustrating the following account. The writer also left a photograph of a little girl, wrapped in a piece of paper on which it is still possible to decipher, in faded pencil writing, the words, 'Baby at the age of two years'. The interest and significance of this portrait, which we reproduce, require no comment.'

These illustrations, eight in number, depict 'Baby' at the age of two, 'Baby on her quarter-deck', 'the bereaved Captain sobbing with his face buried in his hands', and Fosdyk struggling to the platform.

The *Strand's* article was headed:

ABEL FOSDYK'S STORY
TOLD IN HIS OWN WORDS.
(*with a facsimile of a portion of Abel Fosdyk's MS.*)

Fosdyk's story is very long, running to some 12,000 words, and it needs to be condensed considerably. He claimed to have been a member in 1872 of the crew of the *Mary Celeste*, whose name he at least spells correctly, on which vessel he had made previous voyages. He became very friendly with the captain's daughter, whom he names 'Baby'. The vessel experiences rough weather; the strain on Captain Briggs becomes so great that no one dares to approach him. His wife takes to her bed, and in their preoccupation and absence from deck, Baby nearly falls over-board. Fosdyk is permitted to construct a barricade on the bowsprit, which is named 'Baby's quarter-deck', on which she can sit. They encounter a derelict from which the mate rescues one man who dies and fails to save another, his tardiness being criticised by Captain Briggs. The ship gets off course and Briggs (who is in such a state of nervous breakdown that no owner would have entrusted his ship to him for five minutes, observes Fosdyk) finds himself near the Canary Islands. He breaks down completely, pacing the deck like a wild animal, none daring to speak to him. The ship enters an area of calm which, tells Fosdyk, brought the final catastrophe.

The disaster arose out of some conversation of which he did not hear the beginning, he says. It resulted, it seems, from some sneering remarks made by the captain about the mate having failed to enter the water to save the man on the derelict. The remark rankled with the mate and 'now for what took place', Fosdyk continues. Scarcely had the sun got up when the trouble began, he explains. He goes on to tell:

> I went down into the cabin to fetch the basin which Baby used for her porridge. Mrs Briggs had used it for some posset the night before for herself. She came out and gave it to me, and at the same time asked me to get her a can of hot water. I took the basin and brought down about half a pail of warm water. I remember putting a cruet on the table and also one plate which had evidently had nothing but bread on it and was lying on a locker. I went up again, and in something less than half-an-hour returned with Baby's porridge, some bacon, and two or three bits off a knuckle of ham: I cannot call them slices so much as pickings, as there was very little left on the bone. On entering the cabin I saw at once the captain was again in his strange, irritable, and also irritating, mood, and bent on quarrelling with somebody.
>
> 'It's no good, Harry', I heard him say as I entered, 'if you were to talk from now till Doomsday you would never make me say it wasn't a cowardly action.'
>
> 'You needn't be so free with the word "coward" ', replied the mate; 'it isn't a pleasant one, and you seem to have forgotten,

as I told you before, I was fully dressed and in all my clothes, and though one can keep afloat and move a bit, one can't really swim in one's clothes; not really to call it swimming, that is.'

'What!' shouted the captain, 'you mean to say a man can't swim in his clothes?'

To cut a long story short, the captain and mate indulge in a swimming race round the becalmed vessel, both fully dressed, and Mrs Briggs, Baby and crew watch from Baby's quarter-deck which collapses under their weight, throwing them into the sea. Sharks appear, and Fosdyk only saves himself by climbing on to Baby's quarter-deck which is floating in the water. Clinging to it, he sees his companions disappear one by one. He tries to regain the *Mary Celeste*, but a sudden breeze wafts her away. Days later, he is washed up on the coast of Africa from where he is taken to Algiers. He returned to England in 1874 and entered the service of Mr Linford.

That gentleman did not vouch for Fosdyk's story, but the London *Daily Express* commented on it, headlined 'ABANDONED SHIP. MYSTERY SOLVED', and described Fosdyk as a man of 'exceptional reticence and self-control'.

By many people Fosdyk's story was accepted as authentic, and Mr J.G.Lockhart says, writing in 1927, 'even in recent years I have found the belief prevailing that the whole mystery had been cleared up in the *Strand Magazine*.'

Whether or not Mr Linford found the MSS, as he stated, or whether he wrote the story himself, is beyond our knowledge, and we may remark only that the literary form wherein an author attributed his story to an ancient manuscript discovered by chance to give it the semblance of authority, was then popular. Both Conan Doyle and Rider Haggard employed it.

Whoever was its author, Fosdyk or Linford, he makes a thoroughly good job of it; for example, he introduces the otherwise unnecessary incident of the shipwrecked crew to provide a reason for the later swimming race, and he successfully accounts for the alleged presence on board of the derelict's boats when she was found abandoned, and he accounts apparently satisfactorily for the curious and baffling marks found on the *Mary Celeste's* bows, which were made, it is implied, by the construction of 'Baby's Quarterdeck'.

Yet, as Mr Lockhart has pointed out, the story is clearly a forgery and an invention. Fosdyk is ignorant of the *Mary Celeste's* true tonnage, 282, which he names as 600, he increases the ship's compliment to fourteen, whereas it was ten, he supplies the name of seamen, none of whom signed on in New York, he himself takes the place of the actual steward or cook, and he gives the age of the child as seven to eight. The *Mary Celeste* is buffeted by storms in October and November, despite the fact recorded in shipping publications that she sailed from New York on 7 November. On the other hand Abel Fosdyk, or Mr Linford, has clearly read Conan Doyle, for we find a hint that the ship is off course and far to the south, and he appears to have some knowledge of the newspaper item which was published in May, 1873, recording the discovery near Spain of decomposed bodies on a raft.

The true weakness in the story lies in its explanation of how and why the people of the *Mary Celeste* left their ship. On this point Mr Lockhart comments:

> When we look at the story of the disaster, we find it so fantastic that, even if all of Fosdyk's facts that can be verified were true, which they are not, we should remain incredulous. It is not very likely that any captain, even if his nerves were in a bad state, would want or be allowed by his men to go for a swim in the middle of the Atlantic with his clothes on; the overthrow of ten people in the collapse of so small a platform as 'Baby's quarterdeck' a little too convenient to be convincing; and the idea that a man could drift in a clumsy rate, without sail or oar or food or water, from the Azores to the African coast, and survive the experience, is merely ridiculous. The narrative is full of weaknesses such as these, and this is perhaps the reason – no other appears – why Fosdyk chose to carry his secret with him to the grave rather than risk the ridicule of a sceptical public.

Finally Mr Lockhart remarks that:

> Either Fosdyk must have forgotten his sea jargon, or else that Mr Linford, after carefully expurgating any expression of a nautical turn, must have substituted his own wording. We find such phrases as 'No boat of her size', 'We heaved to', 'Got over quite a lot of ground' and 'Had prepared the storm fore and aft mainsail'. Without being so outspoken as the retired mariner whose comment on the story after reading it was, 'The fellow who wrote that doesn't know a poopdeck from

a jib down-haul' we may observe that these are the kind of trifles that betray.

But Abel Fosdyk, or Mr Linford, had at least contributed to the joy of the occasion. The missing captain and crew of the abandoned derelict had indulged, at breakfast time, in an early morning bathe, in a swimming race in mid-Atlantic in mid-winter. A sudden gust of wind left them struggling in the sea as they watched their ship wafted away.

As a 'survivor's story', Abel Fosdyk's 'Yarn' did nothing to solve the mystery. But it certainly improved the Great Legend, now becoming a Myth as impervious to attack and as entrenched in popular regard as the 'Iron' mask which is universally claimed to have disguised the face of Louis XIV's myterious prisoner.

8

Specioti tells his tale and Triggs goes one better

No sooner had the *Strand* published Abel Fosdyk's yarn than it was followed into print by the *Nautical Magazine* which presented an even more lurid solution in its December issue, one which its Editor explained had been sent in by Captain D. Lukhamanoff – 'the well-known agent of the Russian Volunteer Fleet at Hong Kong'. It had been told to him by an old Greek sailor in 1884, Captain Lukhamanoff announced.

The story told by Demetrius Specioti was no more than a variation of the 'pirate' theory, advanced before 1900. Its interest, as that of Triggs' yarn, lies in the proof it provides of the speculation engendered to account for the disappearance of the *Mary Celeste's* people, who apparently left by some means other than by their own boat, which everyone believed had been found swinging on its davits.

Specioti, Captain Lukhamanoff related, told him he had been a member of the crew of the famous brig which he described as 'a long, sharp, black ship with a rakish stem and masts'. One morning on the voyage to the Mediterranean, not far from Gibraltar, they encountered another brig, also black, with the same kind of rakish stem and masts. The strange brig hoists the signal 'Short of provisions – Starving'. Her boat rows across, at its tiller a dark-faced man with a long beard, wearing a sombrero (a nice touch which identifies him as a Spaniard). When the boat is made fast, six men armed with revolvers spring from beneath a tarpaulin and the *Mary Celeste* is taken. Her crew and passengers are abducted to the strange brig which Specioti recognises as a slaver. (The slave trade, we note, had ended fifty years before the *Mary Celeste* sailed). They are forced to work the ship. One by one the slavers are decimated by fever. The impressed men, led by Specioti, kill the survivors and at that moment the slaver is struck by a big ocean steamer which cuts her in two. Specioti only is saved. To enquiries as to the name of his ship, he replies with all kinds of nonsense, being unwilling, he told Captain Lukhamanoff, to tell the true story because he thought no one would believe him.

Specioti's story no doubt earned him numerous drinks in the sea ports of the world. Its publication in 1913 completed that particular cycle of *Mary Celeste* legends and in the next ten years people had other things to think about. But the drifting derelict was not forgotten, and the Great Game, now almost exclusively a British pastime, of solving the Mystery of the *Mary Celeste*, or the '*Marie*' *Celeste*, as most people insisted on misnaming her, re-started in 1924, with the publication, on 24 September, of an article by the London *Daily Express* which announced itself able to offer 'the real solution to the mystery of the *Marie Celeste*, the classic sea mystery which for fifty years has baffled investigators in every part of the world.'

GREAT SEA MYSTERY CLEARED UP
(it headlined)
WHAT HAPPENED TO THE MARIE CELESTE
DERELICT GOLD
CREW'S ESCAPE WITH STOLEN £3,500

Captain H. Lucy, announced the newspaper, whose name was well known all over the Mediterranean and in Eastern waters, claimed to be the only man living who knew how the *Marie Celeste* was abandoned. He had learned the true facts forty-two years before; but he had been under oath not to divulge them until his informant died. He was now at liberty to speak. The *Daily Express* informed its readers, 'For fifty-two years explanations, some extravagant, have been offered to explain how mother and daughter and eighteen men got away from the ship without leaving a trace'.

The true story had been told him in Melbourne by a man named Triggs, stated Captain Lucy. He had been bosun on the *Marie*

Celeste, he claimed, and he said that, when they were within twenty-four hours' run of the coast of Portugal they sighted a derelict tramp steamer, her name erased by the action of the salt water. In the cabin they found a large iron safe, containing £3,500 in gold and silver. They sank the steamer and returned to the *Marie Celeste* where the loot was divided up, the captain taking £1,200, the mate £600, the second mate £400, and Triggs £300. The remainder was divided amongst the crew. The illegality of their act was discussed and it was decided to sink the *Marie Celeste* and make for Cadiz. But before they could do it, they were spoken to by a vessel, which made the sinking of their ship out of the question.

Triggs's story is so ingenious, and yet so absurd, that parts of it deserve more detailed examination. He continues:

> We then decided to get away from the *Marie Celeste* in the three boats which belonged to the sunk steamer. We painted these boats with the name of a schooner belonging to London, and put our boxes in the boats, with the money and some food and water. There was then a north-east wind blowing. This accounted for the course the deserted *Marie Celeste* was on when sighted by the British barque which took her into Gibraltar.
>
> We arrived in Cadiz, which was about fifty miles distant, early the following day and reported the loss of the schooner whose name we had painted on our boats. We said she had struck a submerged wreck. Our money helped us a lot, and the captain spent freely.
>
> We then split up. Some of the crew went to London by a Spanish fruit boat, the captain, his wife and daughter, the two mates and I went to Marseilles by a Spanish coasting boat. From there I went to Australia. I have seen none of my shipmates since.
>
> Our object in leaving the *Marie Celeste* was to make things look as mysterious as possible, so that we could never be traced.
>
> The reason for abandoning her and separating as we did, was because the captain was afraid that some of the hands might have got drunk in Genoa – our destination – and have spoken about the money which we took from the derelict.

'That', said Captain Lucy, 'is the story told me by this man Triggs. I believe it to be the only true story of the *Marie Celeste*. I saw his papers, which proved that he signed on at Boston aboard the *Marie Celeste*, but I must say that he always covered up his name when he showed it to me. I also believe Triggs knew the name of the derelict from which they took the money, but he never trusted me sufficiently to tell.

'I naturally made private inquiries about him for my own satisfaction, and discovered that he had about £100 in the Bank of Australia. I also discovered that he had lived at the Bay View Hotel, King Street, Melbourne, for about five years without being known to do any work.'

The *Daily Express* stated: 'Captain Lucy has kept this strange story of the sea to himself for more than forty years, during which time he has smiled often to read the elaborate solutions attempted in many parts of the world to explain the mystery of the *Marie Celeste*.'

The *Express* provided its readers with three illustrations: a photograph of Captain Lucy, the *Marie Celeste* under full sail (by courtesy of the *Strand Magazine*), and the deserted cabin with its table laid with the 'partly-eaten meal', showing 'the hurried nature of the crew's departure'.

Triggs's story at once ousted Abel Fosdyk and Demetrius Specioti in popular esteem, and it was hailed as the true solution by a London evening paper which deplored the end of a famous mystery. But it did not go unchallenged, for its publication in New York brought wrathful comments from no less a person than Dr Oliver W. Cobb, Captain Briggs's first cousin, who, in a letter to the *New York Times* which was printed on 26 October, declared it reflected unjustly on Captain Briggs's character. Dr Cobb expanded his letter into an article, entitled 'THE MYSTERY OF THE *MARY CELESTE*', which was published by the Magazine *Yachting Monthly* in August 1925, in which he said:

> In the *New York Times*, Magazine Section, page 2, of Sunday October 12, 1924, there appeared a story purporting to be the *true* story of the Mary Celeste as told by one Triggs to Captain Lucy, R.N.R. As Capt. Benj. S. Briggs of the Mary Celeste was a cousin of mine, and the said story reflects very unjustly upon his character – I have been appealed to as one of the family, to set the record right. Captain Briggs was a Christian

gentleman; he belonged to a family of Ship Masters who lived up to the best traditions of the sea. To represent him as a deserter (in the letter to the *New York Times*, Dr. Cobb described it as 'a criminal deserter') of his ship is to desecrate his memory, and any such statement is resented by the family.'

He proceeded to demolish Triggs's story by indicating its many inaccuracies, pointing out that the *Mary Celeste* was square rigged forward, but had no yards on the main mast, having there a fore and aft mainsail and a gaff topsail like a schooner, thus being a cross between a brig and a schooner or what is called a 'hermaphrodite' brig. There were not eighteen men aboard but eleven, Captain and Mrs. Briggs, their baby girl, two mates, a cook and five sailors. Triggs, here marked, said he signed on in Boston but it is known that the crew were shipped in New York. His story, declares Dr. Cobb, was 'pure fabrication with no supporting evidence whatsoever', and he adds, 'It is not necessary to introduce fiction nor to add to the mystery of this story'. He continued, 'On board a whaler or, maybe, a trader amongst the islands of the Pacific, or it may be on a trans-Atlantic liner, a sailor in the forecastle or an officer on the bridge will light his pipe, and after blowing out two or three puffs of smoke will say, "Well! What do you suppose ever became of the crew of the *Mary Celeste*". Fifty-two years have passed and still the question and no real answer.'

Mr J.G. Lockhart, writing in 1927 (*A Great Sea Mystery*) also had scathing criticisms to make of Triggs's story. He points out that, according to Triggs, the *Mary Celeste*, between 24 November, when the last Log entry placed her off the Azores, and 5 December, when the *Dei Gratia* picked her up, performed the following astounding feat: 'she first sailed east more than nine hundred miles on her proper course, and then after being abandoned, turned round and drifted two hundred miles west to Cape St Vincent and north-west to the latitude where she was eventually found. She did this in ten days, during which a north or north-east wind was blowing'.

And, observes Mr Lockhart, it is remarkable that the derelict steamer, Mr Triggs would have us believe, was floating about, not in unfrequented waters, but plumb in the middle in one of the greatest ocean highways of the world, close to a big port and at the very gate of the Mediterranean. The derelict's name could hardly have been rusted away from both her bow and stern. This derelict, he suggests, presented a problem almost as mysterious as the *Mary Celeste*. Who had abandoned her and why? And what became of her crew? To these questions no answer is given by Triggs, he observes.

The financial aspect of the whole business is equally puzzling. Captain Briggs was a man of some substance, remarks Mr Lockhart. He had a home in New England; he had a job, a wife and family and an unblemished reputation and he owned a third (actually an eighth) of the *Mary Celeste*. Yet, all these assets, tangible and intangible, he was ready to throw away for a paltry £1,200; becoming by his action a wanderer on the face of the earth, unable to return to his home, or to follow his calling, or even to use his own name. A more unlikely bargain can scarcely be imagined, and we can be sure that, even if Captain Briggs had fallen to it, his wife, mindful of her son (who did not accompany them) and her home, would have had something to say.'

Captain Briggs's conduct, after deciding to share out the money, was equally incomprehensible. He is afraid to scuttle the derelict for fear his men might talk in their cups, yet he abandons his own ship, making her ultimate discovery inevitable, which would make sure of setting every tongue in the Mediterranean wagging. Somebody's leg was being pulled, suggests Mr Lockhart, but he refrains from hazarding the opinion whether it was that of Captain Lucy or the Editor of the London newspaper.

There is another 'Survivor story' yet to come, but we may turn aside here to consider two further theories which were advanced in 1926 and 1955.

9

From the absurd to the fantastic

Inevitably the problem of the drifting derelict, her sails set, no sign of damage or violence, her boats intact and not a soul on board, and nothing apparently to account for her abandonment in mid-ocean, became fair game for the particular foible or fad of the moment. In the nineteen-twenties the minds of many people in Britain and the United States, chiefly retired Army officers and middle-aged spinsters, were preoccupied by the horrible thought that the British race, or part of it, was descended from the Lost Tribes of Israel and that the Great Pyramid of Egypt enshrined a Revelation that was peculiar to the Christians, the true inheritors of the 'Adamic Race', whoever they may have been. And in some unexplained way these pious but utterly fallacious beliefs were connected with the Lost Continent of Atlantis which was believed to have sunk beneath the waves ten thousand years ago.

There were no Lost Tribes of Israel and if there had been, it would have been quite impossible for them to have trekked across Europe without racial contamination. The belief that the Great Pyramid, (which was built by Pharoah Cheops at Gizeh as a tomb) foretells the future in years by measurements derived from a 'Pyramid inch' – a unit of measurement which was unknown to its architects – is twaddle, and the absurdity of the theory has been shown by no less a person than the late Sir Flinders Petrie, the great Egyptologist. The Atlantean theory is equally nebulous; geological surveys of the ocean bed have shown that if such a lost continent once existed it

Read the "View Over Atlantis" by J. Michell. Who reverts to these absurd ideas & proves them was engulfed beneath the waves long before man appeared on the earth.

In September, 1926, *The British Journal of Astrology* announced a new theory to account for the disappearance of the *Mary Celeste's* people. They were 'dematerialised' in mid-ocean, declared author Adam Bushey. That was the only solution which could stand every test, he claimed. The ship's company included, he stated, two mysterious individuals which brought her complement to the sinister number of thirteen. She cleared from 'Hell Gate', New York, on the *seventh* day of the *eleventh* month (clearly a sinister conjuncture), and she stood out for the East. Twenty-eight days later she was found derelict. (Mr Bushey improves the half-eaten breakfast by the addition of hot-buttered toast!) A first class mystery. The whole world wanted to know what had happened on 25 November, 1872. The explanation was contained in a riddle, he informed his readers:

> Six thousand years after the Fall in Eden, which happened 56 years after Adam's formation as a White man, *viz*. 4,184.6 B.C., a ship left Hell Gate in the kingdom of the West with a cargo of Spirits for a city of the East. As she sailed the seas she passed over a vanished continent called Atlantis, whose King had once ruled the earth; but because of its wickedness it was sunk, and that ship was emptied of all its beings, its papers and its time measurement when it had indeed passed over Atlantis, so that she had none to guide her and none could tell whence she came nor the time. But there were those who watched and who knew; and so, by the grace of God, she was found by the ship of Israel and taken unto the Rock, and that ship was given a new name, a new captain and crew, a new set of papers, and a new time measurement, and she took her Spirits to their appointed haven. That ship sailed 17 days with her old crew, 11 days with no crew, and she lay 70 days in the hands of strangers, or rather in the hands of Israel, before her rightful owner came out of the West and took her over again.

In that riddle lay the only clue, explained Adam Bushey. The answer lay deep in the heart of the Great Pyramid of Gizeh in the land of Egypt, the divine structure mentioned in the 19th Chapter of Isiah, the inspired designer of which knew that when 4,000 years had passed, the Great King would wake up his faithful servants and rule the Earth. Measurements in the Pyramid proved that would happen in the year 1872, A.D., and the *Mary Celeste* was only one of the mysteries of that fateful year. The Great New Captain had whipped up the eleven souls and two angels from the vessel as she passed over the cesspool of pre-deluvian Atlantis. That was the solution to the mystery of the 'Mary of Heaven', as her name meant, the ship found by 'the Grace of God', and brought to the Rock, the portal to the land of Egypt.

While we may dismiss Mr Bushey's bizarre effusion as an example of the strange effect the mystery of the drifting derelict had on people's minds, questioning only the choice of Captain Briggs and his companions for being singled out as an example of Divine Grace, we need to note that the article shows further progression of the myth in which the seamen's pipes have now become half-smoked and their washing is clearly identified as their underwear, a vital fact not previously recorded.

But we, from our pedestal of post-war scientific knowledge, have no cause to ridicule the credulous out-pourings of the nineteen-twenties, for a theory advanced in the nineteen-fifties is no less incredible. Visits to the earth by people from Outer Space obsessed the minds of millions in the period following Hitler's war. 'Flying Saucers' were seen by thousands. They have now been explained satisfactorily as hallucinations induced by the strains and stresses of the Cold War, but in 1955 they filled the imaginations of millions of Americans and not a few Englishmen. Sooner or later someone was bound to connect the disappearance of the people of the *Mary Celeste* with the Flying Saucer craze. The theory 'SNATCHED INTO SPACE ?' was advanced by Professor M. K. Jessup, Instructor in Astronomy at Michigan University, in the London *Evening News* of 30 August, 1955, the article being condensed from his book *U.F.O.*, published by Arco. The author, explains the Editor, 'develops a theory that many inexplicable disappearances of persons can be accounted for by visitations from Outer Space', and the contribution to the problem was entitled: 'This could explain the Mystery of the *Mary Celeste*.

Advancing his solution to the mystery, Professor Jessup stressed that the derelict's upper rigging had been slightly damaged. Apart from that there was no note of disarray or struggle. The sudden disappearance of people at lonely spots at sea is, he observes, not unusual, and no apparent cause is assignable. He cited several examples and he remarked, 'Damage aloft is a common feature of these events and clearly indicates *activity above the ship* or at least above its decks'. The open seas, he stressed, provide an easy *catching place*, and these disappearances were impossible to explain except as *upwards*. The people on board the *Mary Celeste* were levitated by an intelligent force from *above*, he concluded. What motive the space inhabitants had for kidnapping ships' crews was, he admitted, pure speculation.

So now we know what happened to Captain Briggs, his family and crew! Surely, the spacemen, if they exist, can find something better to do than kidnap ten very ordinary, dull people. One feels that their 'snatching into space' of humans could have been put to far better purpose.

Having considered these highly imaginative theories *en bloc*, we can return to the progress of the myth, where another 'survivor' of the derelict's crew awaits our attention.

10

The great Pemberton hoax

The fourth and final 'survivor' story is apparently far more carefully documented than the tales and yarns of Fosdyk, Specioti and Triggs, and, because of the remarkable welcome it received at the time of its publication, it requires far more detailed examination; particularly as it was accepted by many people as the true solution to the Great Mystery of the Sea.

In its issue of July, 1926, *Chambers's Journal*, which had published an article on the famous mystery in 1904, presented its readers with:

THE TRUTH ABOUT MARIE CELESTE
A SURVIVOR'S STORY
BY LEE KAYE

The author began his article:

> Here follows the true story of the brig *Marie Celeste*, and an exact and complete explanation of the mystery which has hung round her name.
>
> On 7th December 1872, at ten o'clock in the morn, a vessel was sighted in the Atlantic sailing along with a full spread of canvas towards the Spanish coast. As she did not respond to signals, and showed no signs of life when viewed through the glasses, the skipper of the hailing vessel despatched a boat's crew to investigate. The stranger proved to be the brig *Marie Celeste*. There was no one about the deck, and search revealed no one in the cabin. The forecastle was silent and deserted. The

> vessel had been abandoned precipitately for no apparent reason.
>
> But how she had been abandoned was even less apparent. The brig's boats – two – stood firm in their chocks on the roof of the deckhouse. They had never beem moved, it was clear, for the paint where the keels touched the chocks was still an unbroken skin. In the forecastle were five seamen's chests and two canvas kit-bags still containing the outfits of the crew. The galley-range, although raked out, was still hot. A cat was sleeping peacefully on the locker. On a table in the after-cabin a meal was laid. The viands were cold, but three cups of tea which stood by the plates were yet luke-warm. The official 'log' had been written up till 24th November, while the slate 'log' presented the appearance of having been hastily cleansed of inscriptions in chalk. Whatever had been written on it was rubbed into a white haze.

'These are the plain facts as recorded by the captain of the finding vessel', states Mr Kaye. It was surmised, he says, that the '*Marie*' *Celeste* had been abandoned on 24 November, and had been drifting unmanned for a fortnight. But he goes on to say: 'this was at once controverted by the fact that she was plainly shaping a course'. Mr Kaye points out:

> The evidence of the warm tea in the cabin and the still hot range in the galley implied that she had been manned to within half an hour of her finding. Further elaborations of the facts – in statements of the crew which boarded her – complicate the story. One account states that the ship's chronometer was missing, which gave rise to a theory that the crew had left the *Marie* under stress of weather and taken the chronometer to navigate the boat or boats. But the boats were still in their chocks, which demolished this theory very effectually. It is recorded that a glass of water which stood on a sideboard in the cabin was still full, showing that the vessel had not encountered heavy weather since it was placed there.

Altogether 'a very pretty mystery of the sea' Mr Kaye observes. Were these all the known facts, the 'mystery' would outlast mankind itself, he suggests. Clearly Mr Kaye is preparing the reader for a new and startling solution to the famous mystery, and in his next paragraph he states: 'there is still living one member – possibly two – of the crew.'

There follows the story told to Mr Kaye by John Pemberton who claimed to have been the cook on the *Mary Celeste* on her famous voyage. Two years later, in 1929, Pemberton's story appeared in book form, published as *The Great Mary Celeste Hoax*, and written by Laurence J. Keating. Lee Kaye and Laurence Keating are assumed by the critics of their publications to have been one and the same man, one name or the other being a pseudonym for the true author. Who Mr Keating, which is assumed to be the author's real name, was, I have been unable to discover but internal evidence found in his publications suggests that he was a Liverpool man. That Kaye and Keating were one and the same is suggested by the fact that the author of the book reacted to criticisms of his article by correcting mistakes, such as that of misnaming the ship the '*Marie*' *Celeste*. On the other hand he became more daring in his statements of facts which had not been challenged. In the article in *Chambers's Journal*, the *Mary Celeste* is made to sail from New York on 7 October, being preceded by the *Dei Gratia* which leaves that port on 2 October. In the book the date of the *Mary Celeste's* sailing is corrected to 7 November. According to Mr Kaye, the ship's name is changed to *Mary Sellars* which, when spoken by Latins in Brazil, became '*Marie Celeste*' and 'Marie' became 'Mary' during the many repaintings of the ship's name on her stern. In his book Mr Keating offers a far more ingenious reason for the change of name. Captain Winchester renames his ship '*Mary Sellars*', which was the name of Captain Briggs's sweetheart, to please him.

John Pemberton's story, told briefly in 1926 and in far fuller form in 1929, is given below, but first we need to notice Mr Kaye's concluding words in 1926 'such, then, is the true story of the brig *Marie Celeste*, and an exact and complete explanation of the "mystery" associated with her', a claim on which the *New York Herald Tribune* of 26 July, 1926, commented, 'So runs the tale of Pemberton, the erstwhile cook, and there are none to dispute the truth of his story' and adding, rather sorrowfully, 'but he damaged a noteworthy mystery by telling it'.

Mr Keating in his 'First Words', as he called his prologue, and in his early chapters, states certain facts about the *Mary Celeste*, the finding of her by the *Dei Gratia*, the proceedings at Gibraltar and the ship's early history, which lead up to Mr Pemberton's arrival on the scene in 1870. He is a member of the crew on the ship's famous voyage to Genoa The rest of Mr Keating's book, over 150 pages, consists of the author's rendering of Pemberton's story which has been called the 'most plausible' of all the solutions to the mystery.

Considerable difficulty arises in properly assessing Pemberton's story as presented by Mr Kaye and/or Mr Keating, due to the author's method of presenting it – in a form in which he leaves the reader in doubt when he is quoting Pemberton and when he is drawing upon outside sources of information. Thus statements which appear to corroborate Pemberton's story may be Pemberton's own 'recollections'. Nor does Mr Keating give us the authority for many of his own statements, which are at variance with the official record.

Mr Keating begins his book with the bringing into Gibraltar on 13 December, by a crew from the *Dei Gratia*, of the derelict found 'more than a week before, not far from the coast of Spain'. Disturbing discoveries are made by the Queen's Proctor and others, which suggest that a crime of violence had occurred on board the brig and that guilty or hunted men had abandoned her in a panic. The most exhaustive inquiry fails to throw any light on the matter and 'every conjecture is at fault'. How the vessel could have been abandoned in mid-ocean becomes a great legend, the sea's most insoluble puzzle which, Mr Keating tells us, 'has baffled three generations to explain.'

According to Mr Keating, the *Mary Celeste* was said to have been found sailing on 'a marvellously direct course' towards her known port of call, Gibraltar, and 'she apparently had been doing so for no less than ten days, which was the most extraordinary feature of the occurrence, because although the people of the *Dei Gratia* stated that they discovered the crew's effects and many valuables and even a fresh breakfast from which persons had apparently just risen, they found evidence in the log that for ten days she had not a soul on board.'

Mr Keating states that 'what the finders said about the condition of the derelict is indelibly set down in the record of their evidence, given before the Chief Justice's Court at Gibraltar' and he implies that he has consulted 'these records and other official matter' by saying that they are preserved in the Registry of the Supreme Court at Gibraltar. He refers to the Report prepared for the 'Privy Council of the British Board of Trade' by Mr Solly Flood whose activities, he declares, were 'robust and frantic'. He it was, states Mr Keating, who developed the first theory of violence and bloodshed and 'who converted a salvage inquiry into a chase after murderers'. The author mentions also 'varying accounts of his strenuous blood hunt', which are to be found in contemporary newspapers such as the *Gibraltar Chronicle*, *Globe*, *Liverpool Mercury*, etc., and in various American Shipping and Commercial Journals, and he refers to the existence in American Archives of four dispatches from U.S. Consul Sprague of Gibraltar, and of two exhaustive personal surveys of the vessel.

'On these established basic foundations' Mr Keating says, 'Many a fantastic edifice has been erected and shattered to atoms again; thousands of people have gone over the ruins with searchlights, seeking to fill up the gap of what happened on board the *Mary Celeste* from the time when she left New York as a brig till the time when the *Dei Gratia* was stated to have picked her up as a brigantine, abandoned and derelict.' But, according to Mr Keating, 'The searchlights have been turned in the wrong direction, the busy rakes have never succeeded in clearing the rubbish'. Bunglers and 'follow-our-leaders' have made the affair of the *Mary Celeste* a greater mystery after fifty years than even the baffled court found it after fifty days. The classic mystery will now be explained, he says.

The veil will be lifted by a man who was on board on that celebrated voyage, he states. The belief that there were no survivors is erroneous. The survivor, he says, whose account is incorporated, was the cook of the *Mary Celeste* 'who is now 80 years of age, and has already given an account of himself to the proper authorities.'

Having thus stated the basic foundation of his book, Mr Keating acknowledges the assistance he has received from certain people in America, and he particularly names the firm of Thorvald, Weiland and Powell, stevedores of New York, and Signor Dominic Malarangi of Genoa 'who has settled an old and fiercely debated argument about the nature of the *Mary Celeste's* cargo', neither of whom appear in the official records of the voyage, it may be remarked.

Mr Keating commences his first chapter by quoting, as the first 'official' notice of the arrival at Gibraltar of the *Mary Celeste*, a report in the Liverpool *Albion*, printed about Christmas time, 1872, 'the source of which' he says 'we cannot trace, but which was issued from Malaga and was stated to be the Spanish Government's production'. The *Albion*, he says, gave a detailed account of:

> how the *Mary Celeste* was discovered tacking suspiciously towards the Spanish coast in the fairway to Gibraltar by Spanish coastguards, who put out from Cadiz, on 6th December, 1872. The coastguards were on the watch for foreign vessels running guns for Carlist insurgents who were engaged in a revolt, and they visited the *Mary Celeste* because she was shaping inshore. The coastguards found the *Mary Celeste* abandoned – her people had either got ashore in the early morning or else had been taken captive by Barbary pirates and, finding no contraband on board her, the coastguards took the derelict towards Gibraltar. The notice went on to say that the coastguards left the brig lying off the Point at Tariffa, the British vessel *Dei Gratia* then being in sight, and that the British shipmaster there sent his prize crew on board. This extraordinary story gains some confirmation through the report of the Spanish lighthouse-keepers at Tariffa, that they had observed, on 12th December, the people of the *Dei Gratia* make two visits by boat to the derelict and that the second party had taken her away. The coastguards went ashore in their own skiff. As six days had thus elapsed one wonders what the Spaniards had been doing with the brig in the interval, and why they should hand her over to the *Dei Gratia*, and was it only coastguards who went off in the skiff.

Mr Keating's report of the discovery of the vessel by Spanish coastguards did *not* appear in the Liverpool *Albion* (the files of which have been examined), as he alleges. Where he found it, or if he found it at all, it is now impossible to say, but it seems that some such incorrect statement must have appeared somewhere for, we recall, Mr J.L. Hornibrook (*Chambers's Journal*, September, 1904) states that the abandoned brig was found in the Straits of Gibraltar by the Spanish authorities.

Whatever 'substance' was contained in this Spanish 'official' notice, Mr Keating observes that it was not confirmed by Captain Morehouse and his men whose story, he says, can be 'substantially reconstructed by consulting the documents endorsed "Minutes of

Evidence Given During Claim For Salvage Proceedings Regarding The Mary Celeste, brigantine of New York." ' The captain of the *Dei Gratia*, claims Mr Keating, produced his log entry relating to the discovery of the derelict which read:

> At ten o'clock on the morning of 4th December, I sighted a sail to the N.E. around Latitude 37N, Longitude 18W. I overhauled her and found her to be a 'brig' of round about 300 tons. She did not answer my signal, and getting closer, I noticed she was swagging all over the place. I thought something was wrong. She was half a mile away. I watched her through my binoculars and I was astonished to see the wheel unmanned, no lookout being kept and in fact nobody on deck at all [an entry, we may remark, which does *not* appear in the *Dei Gratia's* log].

According to Mr Keating, Captain Morehouse went on to say:

> that the strange ship was bowling along under all canvas, standing on the starboard tack, shaping a course towards the Spanish coast. His own ship was on the port tack; the wind was fresh and from the north. He told a story about a long, stern chase and said that he could not come up with the other until three p.m. sea time the following day, when the brig ran off a point and lost way. He was thus enabled to get near enough to give her the hail, 'Do you want assistance?' There was no answer, and there being again no signs of life on board, Captain Morehouse decided to send away a boat to ascertain what was wrong on board the other. He gave the position of this happening as around Latitude 38N, Longitude 17W, at 3 p.m., sea time, on 5th December, 1872.

If Captain Morehouse's evidence was true, Mr Keating points out that the Spanish notice was demolished, for the latitude and longitude given indicated a spot 400 miles due west of Lisbon.

In the evidence he gave to the Vice-Admiralty Court, claims Mr Keating, Captain Morehouse said that while this finessing was going on a 'tramp steamer' sailed round the lee of the strange brig, crossed the *Dei Gratia's* bows and went away. He was able to say that this steamer was a German and that she was bound for the West Indies. He could not state her name; he did not inform her people that he had been chasing the brig since the day before, because the German steamer was three miles away.

The mate of the *Dei Gratia*, asserts Mr Keating, said in his evidence that he thought someone must be aboard the vessel, because he found their breakfast on the cabin table and it seemed to him that these persons had risen just before he entered and had run away, for they had made a start on the food while three cups of tea, untouched, were warm to his thumb. But he could find no one on board. Some washing (three shirts) were found drying on a line in the forecastle and there were pipes and tobacco lying about. The brig had a list to starboard. One of his men drew his attention to the galley and demonstrated to him (by spitting on it) that, though the fire had been raked out, the stove was still quite hot. In a stew pan still on the stove was a chicken, which the men wanted to eat and, the mate is reported to have said 'there was a pussy in the galley; she was asleep on the top of the locker'. He forbade the men to eat the chicken and tossed it overboard, as he thought the derelict was a 'plaguer'. There were no rats on board and he concluded that a plague, probably cholera, coming from foul water, had decimated the vanished company 'who had been dumped one by one, or had somehow in their agony fallen over the bulwarks'.

Mr Keating has not finished with the mate's surprising discoveries on the abandoned ship, which he describes picturesquely as being bellowed across the water to Captain Morehouse. These are too numerous to detail in full but we note that the slight depression found on the bed was attributed by the mate to having been made by a cap, and a sheet of paper with additions worked out on it was discovered in the mate's cabin, which proved not to be a dead reckoning but a totting up of seamen's wages. No reason could be found why or how the missing people could have left the ship. The last entry in the Log had been made at 11 a.m. on 24 November and it showed that the *Mary Celeste* had then been around Longitude 36N and Latitude 27W, in fair weather. The *Dei Gratia* is described as having spent over a day chasing the derelict and was only able to get near to her when she ran off the point at 3 p.m. on 5 December. The second mate, not Deveau who is named as the first mate, takes her into Gibraltar.

Such is Mr Keating's reconstruction of the finding of the *Mary Celeste*, according to him, as stated in evidence at the court at Gibraltar. Captain Morehouse is described as being under the 'stolid assurance' that his claim for salvage will be settled out of hand, without inquiry. No further investigation would have been made, explains Mr Keating, had not the Queen's Proctor been impressed by Mate Deveau's tale of the untouched breakfast in the derelict's cabin and the coincidental presence of the mysterious tramp steamer which had sailed round the *Mary Celeste*.

It may be as well to state here that none of the statements attributed to these witnesses are to be found in the official Transcript of Evidence, which Mr Keating professes to have examined. The author is merely repeating mis-statements from the legend which had built up a picture of the *Mary Celeste*, abandoned with her boats intact, a half-eaten breakfast in the cabin, no one aboard and no reason for her abandonment. And he improves it by the addition of the mythical tramp steamer and by the assertion that the men of the *Dei Gratia* sighted the derelict on the day before they actually boarded her. He quotes an untrue version of the *Dei Gratia's* log for 4 December. He introduces a long stern chase which never occurred.

The fact that the author introduces John Pemberton's story, which is the authority for his book, with a collection of untruths must necessarily disincline us to accept the story that follows but, as we shall find, the story told at Gibraltar by the officers and men of the *Dei Gratia* is claimed by Mr Keating to have been a pack of lies.

Mr Keating continues and, still claiming to quote official documents, he refers to the surveys of the ship and the discovery of the sword, the blade of which has been wiped, and which 'fitted perfectly into the deep cuts found in the topgallant rail', which had been made with the express purpose of obliterating bloodstains with the deliberate intention to cover up a crime. A feature of the case, says Mr Keating, was the extraordinary conflict of facts with which Mr Solly Flood had to deal, and that official is credited with being specially alarmed because the captain of the brig had gone away undressed, while his wife and daughter had gone clothed, even wearing hats. This, in conjunction with the bloodstained sword, convinced the Queen's Proctor that they had been violently removed, and he formed the belief that the master and his family had been brutally murdered. Though to Mr Flood there was a grave element of doubt about this, because the escaping murderers had taken only valueless papers, he put forward, as sufficient motive for the crime – the fact that one barrel of alcohol had been tampered with. His Report to the Board of Trade shows he did not accept the statement of Captain

Morehouse that the derelict had been unmanned for ten days and he really believed that the crew had gone off in the German tramp which had circled the derelict. 'But Mr Flood cannot prove his suspicions.'

Captain Winchester and a Mr Harvey Pascoe, a gentleman otherwise unknown, representing the owners of the cargo, and Captain Hutchins (not Blatchford), brought to command the *Mary Celeste*, come from New York and give evidence to the court, Captain Winchester's testimony being described as of 'no value' because he declares there was no child on board and he is unaware that Captain Briggs was the father of a child. He supplies a list of the crew, naming the mate as 'Henry Bilson', with fourteen others, and he says these names were on the list supplied to him by the New York Shipping Commissioner. Mr Sprague has also been supplied with a list of these fourteen names but his list does not include the name of Henry Bilson, and it records that Albert G. Richardson was the chief mate of the *Mary Celeste*. Of these fourteen names given by Mr Keating, six are correct, though wrongly spelled. But Mr Keating, as we shall see, claims that none of the men listed were actually on board the *Mary Celeste*. The crew list supplied by the Shipping Commissioner was fictitious, he says.

Captain Winchester accepts Captain Morehouse's story and does not contest his salvage claim. Solly Flood considers his attitude as wilful opposition to his inquiry though 'Dr Paton's' analysis (meaning Dr Patron) fails to support his theory of mutiny and murder. Neither the cargo, which is described by Mr Keating as only partly of alcohol, the bulk of it being whale-oil, or the ship, according to Mr Keating, are insured, and the *Mary Celeste* arrives back in Boston in June (not in September), where she is immediately sold by Captain Winchester, followed at once by the *Dei Gratia* which ties up astern. Captains Winchester and Morehouse are described as being on friendly terms.

Mr Keating presents the previous history of the *Mary Celeste*, mis-stating her place of origin and the date on which she was actually acquired by Captain Winchester, and he describes her in 1872 as in poor condition. Captain Winchester is alleged to be in financial trouble and Captain Briggs, after he has acquired a share in the ship, is shocked by his discovery of the state of the principal owner's finances. This brings us to October, 1872. Mr Keating now corrects Mr Kaye's mis-statement that the *Mary Celeste* sailed from New York early in October, but he brings her from Philadelphia, instead of correctly from Boston, early in September.

The rest of Mr Keating's book describes what happened on the fateful voyage through the eyes of John Pemberton, who is identified by Mr Lee Kaye writing in 1926, as 'now 70 years of age, a naval pensioner of the American Civil War', and one of the two still living members of the famous derelict's crew. The other is said to be a Jack Dossell, her boatswain, and both are stated to be residing in England. Mr Pemberton, says Lee Kaye, 'who retains his memory unimpaired' and who possesses 'discharge certificates which place his *bona fides* beyond dispute' joined the *Mary Celeste* on 14 October, 1870.

Mr Keating tells us that John Pemberton was born in Bolton Street, Liverpool, the son of the 'Bold Street crossing sweeper', on 1 October, 1847 (which made him over eighty) and he details his experiences as a seaman from 1860 until 1870, when he was persuaded to ship on the *Mary Sellars* by a boarding house keeper to whom he was heavily in debt. The ship is renamed the *Mary Celeste* and her master, Briggs, is described as being 'a moody man, hard to please'. Henry Bilson becomes her mate. 'Few men made a second trip on the *Mary Celeste*' Pemberton discovers. She was an unhappy ship, making very poor pay-offs, and consequently she was always in the hands of crimps. Pemberton is stated to have made three voyages to Brazil and to have been the cook on the celebrated voyage which started on 7 November, 1872. Pemberton, Mr Keating states in 1929, was still living near Liverpool.

The other survivor, Jack Dossell, is stated by Mr Keating to have died near Shrewsbury, England, in 1917. He made no secret of his membership of the crew of the *Mary Celeste*. His story was being sifted, says Mr Keating, when he was lost sight of but 'much of his recollections are available from notes taken and confidences between him and a venerable shipmate who also sailed in the mysterious brig.'

On the ship's arrival at New York early in September, 1872, Captain Briggs immediately pays off his crew, with the exception of the cook, who remains on board as a watchman. In October the cargo begins to arrive, piling up on the wharf where it is allowed to accumulate because there is nobody to put it on board. Captain

Briggs plans to re-engage his discharged crew but he wishes to leave this as late as possible to avoid unnecessary expense. These men are kept together by the mate, Henry Bilson, who is unpleasantly surprised at the bulk of the cargo waiting to be loaded. That is a stevedore's job, he tells Captain Briggs, who does not agree. Bilson tries to coax the men to re-engage on the *Mary Celeste*, but they are not forthcoming and he arouses Captain Brigg's anger by his frequent absences and broken promises. Bilson takes himself and his crew off and finds all of them a better job on another ship.

Captain Briggs engages a new mate, a man he knew previously. No effort is made to load the ship, and no crew has yet been engaged. Fourteen-hundred and eighty casks lie on the wharf awaiting shipment, and it is claimed they will dreadfully overload the ship. The captain goes to his home in New York at night leaving only Pemberton and the new mate, whose name is Hullock, on board. No seaman can be found to engage for the voyage, especially with the prospect of working the huge cargo on shipboard. At last when even more casks arrive, Captain Briggs unwillingly engages a master porter, named William Weiland, to load his ship. Mr Keating quotes Mr Weiland's 'Work Book' to show that 520 barrels of sperm oil, 350 drums of spirit, 50 barrels of alcohol and another 130 barrels of sperm oil were loaded on to the *Mary Celeste*, both under hatches and on deck. This stowage left the brig with an over free-board of only 2½ inches, which was considered safe. But the cargo stowed on shipboard still left a surplus on the wharf.

Close to where the *Mary Celeste* was loading, states Mr Keating, lay moored a British barquentine. She is described as a poor sort of vessel with scarred sides and weathered-off paint and of scurvy appearance; a 'moucher' ship, one that sailed about seeking cargoes where she could. This ship, identified by Mr Keating as the *Dei Gratia*, was unable to get a cargo, he says. 'There is not the slightest doubt that the master of the *Dei Gratia* and the master of the *Mary Celeste* were already well acquainted' states Mr Keating. Captain Morehouse was constantly with his friend on board the *Mary Celeste*, taking his meals with Captain Briggs and even sharing his tobacco. At night the twain had the habit of going away together 'up the town'. The position was this; Captain Morehouse had an empty ship and a complete crew while Captain Briggs had an over-full ship and no crew at all. Very naturally, claims Mr Keating, they arranged the matter to their mutual benefit. If Captain Briggs would let him take the extra cargo he would lend him some of the *Dei Gratia's* crew, suggested Captain Morehouse. He offered to relieve Captain Briggs of a hundred of the barrels, which were stowed as a deckload on the *Mary Celeste*. Captain Briggs benefited in another way also from this deal. It enabled him to take his wife on board for the voyage.

Mate Hullock, says Mr Keating – presumably on Pemberton's authority – 'seems to have been a man of very cautious disposition'. He and Captain Briggs were not strangers to each other, for they had made a voyage together in 1868 on the *Mary Sellars* before her name was corrupted into *Mary Celeste*. There was an old-standing ill feeling between them, now fanned into flame by Briggs's intention to bring his wife with him on the voyage. Mrs Briggs, the erstwhile 'Mary Sellars', according to Mr Keating, had 'had Hullock for a suitor prior to Benjamin Briggs'. Hullock had taken her marriage badly and the author suggests that his employment as mate was due to the influence of Mrs Briggs.

Around 1 November, asserts Mr Keating, the *Mary Celeste* had finished loading but had still no crew. Nominally, he says, the supply of crews for vessels was controlled by the Shipping Commissioner but, he declares, 'this panjandrum' could no more have supplied seaman than he could have walked the tightrope. He could furnish only land lubbers, the scourings of the city's jails. The supply of real seamen was in the hands of the crimps, the boarding house keepers who were, in 1872, holding shipmasters to ransom. Upon being refused a crew by his own particular crimp, Captain Briggs went to the Shipping Commissioner and the names of fourteen men were supplied to him and these fictitious names were, claims Mr Keating, those given to the Court at Gibraltar as the derelict's missing crew. None of them was on board, declares Mr Keating.

By now Captain Briggs had persuaded the shippers of his cargo, which was too large for him, to give the surplus to Captain Morehouse, and in return he asked Morehouse, who had fourteen seamen, more than he needed, to lend him some men. Briggs's trust in Morehouse was 'almost pathetic,' says Mr Keating; for he alleges that Morehouse intended to annexe the whole of Brigg's cargo from his 'evil smelling' ship which, owing to its cargo of whale oil, carried an atmosphere of 'decaying death', that being the reason given why Captain Briggs had failed to recruit a crew. The two captains dine 'over a bottle of whisky' and Morehouse, whom Mr Keating describes as 'muscle-bound inside the scull', agrees to lend Briggs three seamen as far as the Azores where he can ship other men, and where the two ships will rendezvous. Briggs still needs more men and he succeeds in persuading the crimp, Duncan Findlay, to send him some. But Findlay, angry that Briggs has gone behind his back to the Shipping Commissioner, sends him three 'bone breakers'; one a man 'primed to murder', named Peter Sanson, another named Jack Dossell and the third a shanghaied giant called Carl Venholdt.

The crew arrive on the *Mary Celeste* just as Mrs Briggs comes on board with 'Baby', not her child, we learn, but her 'cottage-piano', a musical instrument which we are told is called a 'Baby' in American saloons. 'This new arrival', says Mr Keating, 'was destined to attain historic importance'; and he goes on to say, 'We have here one of the most ludicrous examples of jumping to conclusions that it is possible to conceive.' Mr Flood at Gibraltar, he explains, jumped to the fatuous conclusion that the name implied that a child had been on board and the world has since always assumed the child's presence on the *Mary Celeste*. Mrs Briggs, Mr Keating tells us, was 'near a dwarf', her tiny clothes assisting to create the illusion that there had been a child on board.

The *Mary Celeste* sails on 7 November, Captain Morehouse waving farewell from the quay and reminding Briggs of their assignation at the Azores. There were on board, Mr Keating claims, ten souls, comprising Captain Briggs and his wife, John Pemberton the cook, Toby Jackson Hullock, the mate known as the 'Baltimore bully', the three men sent by the crimp and the three seamen from the *Dei Gratia* who were named Tom Moffat, Charlie Manning, and Billie Hawley.

Trouble started at once. Mate Hullock and the giant Venholdt quickly came to blows and their fights continued off and on for days while the *Mary Celeste* was buffeted by hurricanes. The tiny brig, like a chip in the water, is thrown relentlessly onwards; the piano breaks loose and is lashed up by Hullock; the hurricane rages;

the crew and master and mate are at loggerheads, quarrelling and fighting amongst themselves. After a short spell of fine weather, and while close to the Azores, the *Mary Celeste* is struck by a sudden hurricane squall which takes everyone unawares, Captain Briggs wearing only 'green plush slippers' and Mrs Briggs pounding out hymn tunes on her piano. There comes a terrible gust of wind; the ship is forced on her beam-ends; the piano breaks loose from its lashings and crushes Mrs Briggs against the wall. This happens on 24 November.

Mrs Briggs dies from her injuries next day. Her husband is inconsolable and his brain is so affected by his bereavement that he orders the crew to throw Peter Sanson, whom he holds responsible for his wife's accident, overboard. But instead, the offending piano is jettisoned by Mate Hullock who insists that Mrs Briggs's body be put overboard too. Briggs goes raving mad, locks himself in the cabin and is found, when the door is battered down, sponging the naked body of his wife with 'booze'. Her body is taken by the crew and put over the side, and that night Briggs himself disappears. In a further extension of their running fight, Venholdt, grappling with Hullock, goes over the side too.

The crew are demoralized and take to drink. The three crimp's men fear that their story will not be believed and that on reaching port they will be charged with mutiny and murder. On 29 November the vessel is close to the island of St Maria, from which bumboats row out, manned by fruit peddlers crying, 'Spikkin da Americano'. Mate Hullock, Peter Sanson, and Jack Dossell go ashore in a bumboat, Hullock first 'signing off the crew' and paying them their wages due from the ship's treasury, which necessitates an addition being made on a piece of paper.

The *Mary Celeste* sails on, the three crew men from the *Dei Gratia* seeking their own ship – which is miraculously sighted on 4 December, at 10 a.m. which necessitates the seamen leaving their half-eaten breakfast on the cabin table when they rush up on deck. A conference is held with Captain Morehouse, who decides to pretend that the *Mary Celeste* was an abandoned derelict, and she is brought into Gibraltar where John Pemberton, having been paid his wages and warned of his dangerous position in that, if he talks, he may be charged with murder, is shipped off to England in the steamship *Columbian* on 18 December, reaching Southampton on the 23rd. He sails for the Far East early in January 1873 and he wanders up and down the Seven Seas for many years occasionally meeting up with Hullock, Sanson and Dossell, with whom he laughs at the world's clumsy attempts to solve the mystery of the *Mary Celeste.* No one will believe them when they tell the 'true story'.

In Gibraltar, Morehouse hoodwinks the authorities, who are suspicious but can prove nothing, and he is given a small award, not for salvage, but for 'assisting a distressed vessel at sea', with which he is quite content for as the captain of a 'moucher' – a ship seeking its cargoes where it can – he is used to small pickings.

Such is John Pemberton's story, as disclosed to the world by Mr Keating. That there was an old seaman of that name living in Liverpool, England, in 1929, is proved by an interview with him reported in the London *Evening Standard* on 6 May, 1929, which described John Pemberton as aged ninety-two, and as 'the sole survivor of the brigantine, *Mary Celeste*'. The greatest of all sea mysteries was a sham', declared the newspaper. It was concocted by Captain Morehouse for the sake of the salvage money, and the *Evening Standard* described its story as:

THE LAST SURVIVOR OF THE
MARY CELESTE
tells
A TALE THAT JOSEPH CONRAD
MIGHT HAVE WRITTEN.

What are we to make of John Pemberton's tale, the story which 'damaged the mistery', according to the *New York Herald Tribune*, the truth of which there was no living person to dispute? Writing his 'Last Thoughts' on the *Mary Celeste* in his book, published in 1929, *Strange Tales from the Seven Seas*, Mr J.G. Lockhart calls the Pemberton-Keating explanation 'admirably ingenious' inasmuch as it covered most of the facts and was supported by a wealth of detail.

There can be little doubt that Mr Keating found an old sailor in Liverpool who said he had been a member of the derelict's crew. Pemberton told him his story, one which had probably earned him many pints of beer and had become improved in the telling. Between its first publication and its appearance in book form, Laurence Keating dug into the old files and in them he found the embellishments which gave Pemberton's story a ring of truth. Mr Keating lifted the statement 'that every conjecture is at fault' from the *Liverpool Mercury*. He adopted and improved upon Conan Doyle's intact boats. He accounted satisfactorily for the half-eaten breakfast, repeated J.S.C.'s story of the tramp steamer, worked in the sum in addition on the piece of paper, changed Fosdyk's 'Baby' into a piano, adopted that gentleman's claim that Captain Briggs became insane, and back-dated Mr Bernstein's suggestion of a love affair on board to a previous flirtation.

The fabricated nature of Mr Keating's 'solution' is indicated by another slip. He claims that the *Dei Gratia* sighted the derelict on 4 December and caught up with her next day. In some of the early reports of her discovery, which Mr Keating diligently studied, it was stated that the derelict was found on 4 December. So in fact she was, according to the time reckoning of the *Dei Gratia* which was still keeping New York time. By 'sea time', the date was 5 December. This apparent discrepancy led Mr Keating to think he had stumbled on a new clue, missed by all previous investigators, and he jumped to the conclusion, and found it suspicious, that Captain Morehouse had been following the *Mary Celeste* for twenty-four hours. And, according to Mr Keating, the so-called derelict had quite different sails on her yards on the two days, which, of course, proved that someone was on board.

To accept Pemberton's explanation it is necessary to jettison most of the known facts. Mr Keating alleges that the crew list supplied to the court at Gibraltar was composed of fictitious names. But, as we shall learn in Chapter XII, the composition of the crew, as recorded in the files of the New York Commissioner of Shipping, is corroborated by independent evidence. For example, a man named Edward William Head is listed as the ship's cook, the position Pemberton claimed to have held, and Head's widow wrote from New York to Consul Sprague asking him to send her late husband's effects to her. It is strange, if Mr Keating's crew list is the true one, that none of the men officially listed as members of the *Mary Celeste's* crew was ever heard of again, and that they were mourned for many years by their families. The presence on board of the

Briggs's child is well attested and neither Benjamin Briggs nor David Morehouse bore the disreputable characters attributed to them by Mr Keating – who turns Captain Briggs into an unwholesome maniac and Captain Morehouse into a petty rogue, depicting both men as seedy adventurers. Mrs Briggs was not born 'Mary Sellars'. Her musical instrument was a harmonium, not a cottage piano, and it was found on board the derelict and returned to her husband's brother. It still exists in the possession of his descendants. It did not therefore, as Mr Keating claims, go overboard near the Azores. The seemingly most plausible aspect of Pemberton's story is its inherent suggestion that the *Mary Celeste* was manned when she was found, for this appears to account for the otherwise extraordinary fact that, when found, she was sailing on her exact course and had been doing so for at least ten days. This is a matter we must leave for discussion until the final chapter.

While Pemberton's story is highly improbable, to say the least of it, its greatest weakness lies in the method of its presentation by Mr Keating, who quotes documents he has obviously never consulted, re-states the old myths about the *Mary Celeste*'s condition, which shows he has made no attempt to check up on his facts, and fails to substantiate his specific statements by quoting specific authorities, other than John Pemberton. He sets out to render his story convincing by printing a mass of detail which, while it appears at first sight to corroborate Pemberton's story, has in reality little or no bearing on it. If Pemberton's story were true, it was incapable of corroboration and, realising this, Mr Keating supplies his readers with a wealth of information about ship movements and sailings which he could easily have culled from the files of newspapers in Liverpool, which was probably the city of his origin.

Mr Keating mentions one particular detail by which it seems possible that Pemberton's story can be corroborated, but in printing it he probably lets the cat out of the bag. He states that Pemberton was shipped from Gibraltar on 18 December in the *Columbian* which reached Southampton on the 23rd. Shipping records show that the *Columbian* did just that in 1872. Pemberton, in all probability, was a member of her crew. While his ship lay at Gibraltar he may have heard the story of the drifting derelict which had been brought in on the 13th, about which everyone was talking, and he invented his story, placing himself on board the *Mary Celeste* as her cook. Then he met Mr Keating who built it up for him into the 'Great *Mary Celeste* Hoax' or, as I prefer to call it, 'The Great Pemberton Hoax'.

Pemberton did not sail on the *Mary Celeste*. That fact is established without question or doubt from the records. Nor did he ship on her under the assumed name of Edward Head. The nearest he came to the *Mary Celeste* may have been the sight of her in Gibraltar roadstead.

Pemberton's story brought Mr Arthur Briggs, the son of Benjamin Briggs, and Dr Oliver Cobb, his cousin, hot foot into print to refute it in the *Boston Post* on 8 August, 1926. Mrs Priscilla Richardson Shelton, sister of the *Mary Celeste's* chief mate, Albert Richardson, interviewed by the *New York Herald Tribune*, on 29 July, 1929, expressed her scepticism of Keating's story and she called Pemberton an imposter. Given an opportunity to reply to the many criticisms levelled at his story by the *New York Times* Book Review of 13 October, 1929, Mr Keating could do no more than lamely claim that his 'piano' was not the same as the 'melodeon' and he reasserted his statement that Mrs Briggs had been Mary Sellars and that there was no child on board.

Pemberton's story had its vogue for a time amongst those keeping a track on 'Mary Celestiana' but, like the other pseudo-survivor stories, it was dismissed as fraudulant by all responsible critics, the number of whom, as we shall see in the next chapter, was now increasing.

11

Keeping an even keel

The spate of words, legendary, mythical, fraudulent, absurd and fantastic, is not yet finished and only in the nineteen twenties did more sober thoughts begin to challenge the falsifications of the myth-makers and imposters. But imagination had nearly run its course. Nearly every possible or impossible solution to the mystery had now been ventilated and it remained only for Mr H.T. Wilkins, a fervid searcher after buried treasure in print and a chronicler of piratical deeds, to 'solve the mystery' by suggesting, in the *Quarterly Review* of July, 1931, that the captain and crew of the *Dei Gratia* were guilty of murder, or that at least grave suspicion attached to them, a theory which is referred to in Chapter XV.

Next, in order of appearance, Mr J.L. Hornibrook who, we recall, advanced the giant octopus theory in 1904, reappeared in *Chambers's Journal* in March 1933 with a less scientific but perhaps a more romantic solution. Announcing 'New Light' on the mystery, he had nothing more startling to suggest than the hoary tale of piratical attack. The *Mary Celeste* had been seized, and her people taken captive, by a Moorish craft, manned by Riff pirates who, according to the author's seafaring informant, Captain J.L. Vivian Millet, were still active in the early eighteen seventies. 'The blow had fallen within the last few hours' before the *Dei Gratia* found the derelict, stated Mr Hornibrook.

As the nineteen twenties and thirties progressed, numerous news-paper and magazine articles revived the famous mystery or reviewed the current survivor stories, nearly all of them supporting the edifice of the Great Myth by incorrectly stating the facts (which was by now a fully established practice) thereby helping to perpetuate the errors and fallacies which had grown like barnacles around the drifting derelict. Keeping to approximate chronological order, the next addition to the legend was supplied by Captain Arthur Crocker, a Hull barge skipper, who claimed in the London *Daily Herald*, on 17 May, 1937, that the *Mary Celeste* was boarded, shortly after she had been abandoned, by the crew of the *Kentishman*, on which he was cabin boy, and he stated he still possessed documents taken from her cabin. Captain Crocker's object in coming forward after this lapse of time was to claim reward for salvage from Lloyds' of London.

Another author, Mr W. F. Hartin, named the puzzle of the drifting derelict 'The Most Baffling Sea Mystery of All' in the *Sunday Dispatch* on 7 March 1937, and, jumping ahead a little, we find no less a person than Commander Campbell of B.B.C. 'Brains' Trust' fame, declaring in the *Sunday Dispatch* on 19 April, 1942, 'I have Solved the Mystery', telling his readers that when the *Mary Celeste* was boarded the fire in her galley was burning brightly. He supplied a new version of John Pemberton's story, as told to a sailor named Pike in Sydney, Australia. Another equally famous author, Lieutenant-Commander Rupert Gould, R.N., of the Admiralty's Hydrographic Department, who had talked on the radio about the famous mystery, referred to it in 1943 in his collection of broadcast talks entitled *The Stargazer Talks*, in which he reviewed some of the current theories and did his best to correct the most notable errors and misconceptions. Mr J. G. Lockhart did the same in his *A Great Mystery of the Sea*, published in 1927, in which he withdrew his earlier theory, presented in 1924 in his *Mysteries of the Sea*. Writing in 1927, Mr Lockhart says:

> In *Mysteries of the Sea* I put forward a solution which a number of people were kind enough to approve, and which others, perfectly reasonably, regarded as too far-fetched to be permissible. My solution was suggested to me by the horrible and authentic story of the *Mary Russell*, a brig sailing from Barbadoes to Cork in 1828, whose Captain suddenly went off his head and, with the assistance of two apprentices, first bound and

then butchered the greater part of his crew, only two men, both badly injured, managing to escape from him and to hide in the hold. I suggested that the presence of the harmonium and of religious books and music in the cabin of the *Mary Celeste* might possibly be the clue to a similar tragedy; that the Captain, a man of excellent character, might have developed religious mania, and, with the strength and cunning of the homicidal lunatic, have attacked, overpowered and murdered his wife and child and crew, taking them one by one and unawares; and that finally, the mad Captain of an empty ship, he may have recovered his senses, as homicidal maniacs generally do, and, horrified by his crimes, have thrown himself overboard. All this was merely conjecture, of which little more could be said than that, although there was not a jot of positive evidence in its support, it roughly accounted for most of the facts as I have given them.

Despite these attempts by serious authors to put the *Mary Celeste* back on an even keel, tales, strange and wonderous continued to flow from many less eminent and more sensation-seeking writers. But a new accent on truth was beginning to appear, due largely, as we shall see, to the efforts of Dr Oliver Cobb, who as a boy of fourteen in 1872 had been an intimate member of the Briggs family circle. In the August issue, 1925, of *Yachting Monthly* he set out chiefly to refute the story of Triggs, and he stated a number of facts which denied the famous legendary details.

Before turning to see what was or was not stated in the testimony then given by the officers and men of the *Dei Gratia*, let us briefly enumerate the fictions upon which the legend of the drifting derelict rested and upon which 'evidence' the various solutions presented from 1884 to 1940 were based.

When sighted, we are told by the myth-makers, the *Mary Celeste* was under full sail, a long stern chase was necessary by the *Dei Gratia* to catch up with her, a German tramp steamer was crossing her bows, and the sea was calm. When she was boarded there was not a soul on board, yet a half-eaten breakfast stood on the cabin table, three tea cups still warm to the touch, a bottle of cough mixture open on the table, a phial of oil and a thimble standing by the sewing machine in which a child's garment was in the act of being repaired, the Captain's watch hung from a bracket still ticking, the stove in the galley was warm, the galley fire burning brightly, a cat peacefully asleep on a locker, the sailors' pipes half smoked, their washing hanging out to dry, a bloodstained axe, and/or a cutlass, lay on the deck, the ship's boats stood intact on their davits and there was no sign of damage or of violence.

These are the 'unassailable facts' on which the legend is based; the credo or libretto which is stated and repeated time and time again by slavish imitators. To account for these 'facts', because they were apparently inexplicable, it is implied or suggested that the *Mary Celeste's* crew were a gang of cut-throats, thirteen in number, drunken, dissolute and murderous, or that Captain Briggs was a homicidal maniac or a criminal or a bully. Similar aspersions have been cast on the Captain and crew of the *Dei Gratia*, and the size, type and complement of both ships have been variously mis-stated. Captains Briggs and Morehouse are stated to have been friends and their ships are supposed to have been berthed next to each other in New York a few weeks before the *Dei Gratia*, of all ships, found the *Mary Celeste* abandoned in the wastes of the ocean.

We can now examine the official records to see what the 'facts' really were.

12

The ship, the captain & the crew

The *Amazon*, renamed the *Mary Celeste* in 1868, was built at Spencer Island, in the Bay of Fundy, Nova Scotia, in 1861, by Joshua Dewis; the first of twenty-seven similar vessels built by him, being registered on 10 June at Parrsboro, 25 miles away. In her first register she is described as 'brigantine-rigged', meaning that she had two masts, the fore-mast being square rigged, and the main mast 'fore and aft' or schooner rigged. In the records of the Atlantic Mutual Insurance Company she is described as a 'half-brig', having a billet head, which means that she had a carved scroll under the bowsprit, a square stern and, originally, only one deck. She was 'carvel built', having flush planking as against 'clinker built' which implies that the planks of the ship's hull overlap. She was built of birch, beech, maple and spruce woods and the cabins were finished with pine. Her measurements were, length 99.3 ft.; breadth 25.5 ft.; depth 11.7 ft.; gross tonnage 198.2 tons. Mr Charles Edey Fay has collected and printed considerable information about the vessel's building and her early ownership and voyages, which need not concern us here unduly.

On 31 December 1868, the *Amazon* was transferred to American ownership, renamed *Mary Celeste* and registered at New York in the ownership of Richard W. Haines. At that time she had only one deck and two masts, and her registered tonnage was given as 206.28 tons. It appears that she had been wrecked and that Richard Haines had bought her for $1,750 and he spent $8,825.03 on repairs.

Why the name '*Mary Celeste*' was selected for the brig on her change of ownership in 1868 is unknown. Various authors have stated that, to quote Mr J. G. Lockhart, 'her name was soon changed to the *Mary Sellars* which in the course of years and maltreatment by many tongues, was corrupted into "*Mary Celeste*", an odd hybrid of Latin and Saxon.' Mr Keating, on the other hand, is more explicit. According to him, the ship's name was changed to the *Mary Sellars* on 26 March, 1867, when she was registered in the ownership of 'Messrs. Winchester, Hart and Briggs (Master)'. Mr Keating's ingenious version of how the '*Mary Sellars*' became the '*Mary Celeste*' is as follows:

> Around this name Mary Sellars hangs a quaint romance made use of by Winchester to mollify the salty Briggs. On the surface, it is only a typical American ship's name – the United States Register, as is well known, is largely filled with such denominations. But *Mary Sellars* was not merely a euphonious fancy of Mr Winchester's; Mary Sellars, from whom the name derived, was a very real person; no one less than the sweetheart of Captain Benjamin Briggs, who was expected to appreciate the supple compliment. Mary Sellars it is pitiful to reflect, was the unfortunate lady who, as the wife of Captain Briggs, was destined afterwards to disappear with her husband and his crew from the celebrated and mysterious *Mary Celeste*. Her identity is strikingly confirmed, apart from private documents, by well recorded official testimony. In the inventory of the articles found on board the derelict brig at Gibraltar in 1872 are mentioned the books and music sheets which the captain's wife had taken aboard at New York. Some of them were endorsed 'A present to M. Sellars from her sister Alice. Jersey City, 1869.' From this it appears that the Mrs Briggs of 1872, the owner of the music sheets and books, was the M. – most certainly Mary – Sellars of 1869. (As it is thus claimed that this romantic ship master Briggs had not yet wedded his sweatheart Mary Sellars in 1869, it is obvious there did not exist any child aged around 7 or 8, although it is fabled such a one was lost with its parents.)

Mr Charles Edey Fay, the careful documentor of the history of the *Mary Celeste*, makes no such startling claim; and his version, that the reason for the change of name is unknown, is to be preferred. As will be seen later in this chapter, Mr Keating's statements about

Mrs Briggs are not confirmed by the known facts.

On 13 October 1869, the *Mary Celeste* was acquired by new owners, James H. Winchester, Sylvester Goodwin and Danie Sampson, and on 11 January 1870, the new master, Rufus Fowler, also acquired a share, being replaced on 29 October 1872, by Benjamin Spooner Briggs. By that date a number of changes had been made in the ship's construction, as is disclosed by her Register. She was given two decks, in place of one, and her length was increased to 103 ft., her breadth to 25.7 ft., her depth to 16.2 ft. The raising of the level of the deck added to her tonnage – which was now registered as 282.28 tons. Contemporary records, printed by Mr Fay, show that these alterations were effected at the cost of over $10,000, and, as a result, the *Mary Celeste* gave the appearance of being a new vessel. That her condition was first class is suggested by the words of Captain Briggs, who told his mother in a letter written just before his departure from New York 'our vessel is in beautiful trim'.

On her return to New York in September 1873, from her ill-fated voyage to Genoa, the *Mary Celeste's* owners became Captain Winchester and Simpson Hart who transferred his share in her on the same day, 10 October, to John Q. Pratt. On 3 February 1874 we find her registered in the name of Captain Winchester only, and on that date he transferred her to five new owners, in whose possession she remained until 25 February 1880 when she was acquired by a Mr Wesley Grove and several others. The last registration entry in the records of the United States Government is on 4 August 1884 and the register is finally endorsed 'Total Loss By Stranding, 3 January, 1885, on Reefs of Rochelais, near Miragoane Haiti. 7 on board. None lost.'

Mr Kingman N. Putman, a New York surveyor and brother of Major Putman, the publisher, has described his visit to Haiti, at the request of the underwriters, in the *Nautical Gazette*, 31 December, 1913. The suspicions of the underwriters about the loss of the *Mary Celeste* had been aroused, apparently, by divergencies in the cargo manifest: which showed that of her cargo of beer, more bottles had been billed to a barrel than a barrel could hold. On arriving in Haiti, Mr Putman rode on horseback from Port-au-Prince to the port of Miragoane to which the *Mary Celeste's* rescued crew had been taken. Her captain, Gilman C. Parker, he learned, had sold the ship's cargo, which had been salvaged and which was insured for $30,000, to U.S. Consul Mitchell for the sum of $500, and Mitchell claimed to have lost money on the deal. When Putman opened a case shipped as 'cutlery' and insured for $1,000 he saw why. 'It contained', he says, 'dog collars worth about $50. Cases insured as boots and shoes contained shoddy rubbers worth about 25 cents each.' The bottles of 'beer', he found, were filled with nothing stronger than water.

Clearly the loss of the *Mary Celeste* was a put-up job and the insurance claims were fraudulent. Mr Putman took the evidence to New York and he returned to Haiti as a Deputy United States Marshal armed with powers to subpoena witnesses and to order Consul Mitchell and Captain Parker to return to New York for trial, the latter on charges of conspiracy and barratry, the wilful wrecking of a vessel, an offence punishable by death under the laws of the United States. He secured the arrest of Parker but Mr Mitchell was more elusive. At Miragoane a Haitian General informed him that the Consul was about to take to the woods and the President of the Republic had instructed him to capture him and hand him over – an offer Mr Putman found it prudent to refuse on the grounds that he was travelling on a British ship, on which, because it was not allowed to carry passengers, he was listed as 'Chaplain', and the abduction from Haitain territory of an American citizen might lead to international complications. Mr Mitchell was allowed to remain in the woods.

Captain Gilman Parker was arraigned in court in Boston on 20 April 1885, and he was committed to appear in the Circuit Court on 15 May to answer the charge. Testimony was then given that when the *Mary Celeste* struck 'it was a clear day and the sea was smooth; that the reef on which the vessel struck was plainly marked on the chart and clearly visible' and that 'the wheelman saw the reef, changed his course, and, on the captain's orders, immediately set it back, with the result that the vessel went on the centre of the reef.' It was testified also that 'what was practically a dummy cargo of fish, rubber soles, etc., were put on board and heavily insured.' The total insurance amounted to $25,000. Mr Putman says, 'The shippers confessed the part they had played; they had consigned goods of little or no value, grossly over-insured and had induced Captain Parker to run his ship aground so that she became a total loss and they were able to claim from the insurance companies. One firm in particular had recovered no less a sum than $5,000 on a load of rotten fish.'

According to Mr Putman, the jury at the first trial disagreed and Captain Parker died while awaiting a new trial, as did the first mate who had given evidence against him. One of the shippers committed suicide and all the firms concerned in the fraud failed, 'part of the strange fate', Mr Putman observes, 'which appeared to pursue anyone who had anything to do with the business.'

That was the unfortunate end of an unfortunate ship. We can turn now to consider the facts relating to her captain and crew in 1872, men who have been shown, as Mr J.G.Lockhart observed, 'to put it mildly in what can only be described as a most unfortunate light'. Captain Briggs, he points out, has been represented as 'a bully, or a swindler, or a homicidal maniac.' The names of the alleged drunken, dissolute, and murderous crew, declared to number 13, have been variously given by the myth-makers. The records of the New York Shipping Commissioner (National Archives, Washington D.C., Records of Department of the Treasury, Bureau of Customs) show by the Articles of Agreement signed on 4 November 1872, the *Mary Celeste's* ships company consisted of:

Master: Benjamin Spooner Briggs.
Crew: Albert G.Richardson, aged 28, born Maine, wages $50 a month.
Andrew Gilling, aged 25, born New York, wages $35 a month.
Edward William Head, aged 23, born New York, wages $40 a month.
Volkert Lorensen, aged 29, born Germany, wages $30 a month.
Arian Martens, aged 35, born Germany, wages $30 a month.
Boz Lorensen, aged 25, born Germany, wages $30 a month.
Gottlieb Goodschall, aged 23, born Germany, wages $30 a month.

Both mates (Richardson and Gilling), the steward Edward Head, and the four seamen, drew a month's wages in advance.

That the two mates, steward and four seamen who signed the

Articles of Agreement were in fact the men who sailed on the *Mary Celeste's* famous voyage is attested by other sources. All were assumed to have been drowned at sea in November-December 1872 by their relatives who, in certain cases, are known to have mourned their loss for years, facts which belie the suggestion that any of the ship's company survived, or that the crew was composed of quite different men.

As regards the first mate, Albert Richardson, Mr Fay has discovered a document on file at the Veteran's Administration Bureau at Washington which is the joint affidavit of James H. Winchester and Joseph Noyes, stating that 'Albert G. Richardson sailed in our employ for about two years and the said Albert G. Richardson was lost, drowned from our brig *Mary Celeste* on or about November 24, 1872.' This affidavit, suggests Mr Fay, supported Mrs Richardson's application for a pension, which she was granted and which she received until her death on 29 April 1937, at the age of 91.

In respect of the second mate, Andrew Gilling, a letter on file shows that the Pastor of the Parish of Kathy, Samso, Denmark, wrote to the Danish Consul at Gibraltar on 8 July 1873, enquiring on behalf of his 'bereaved and sorrowful mother' and asking for news of his fate.

The Articles of Agreement show that the cook and steward of the *Mary Celeste* was named Edward William Head, not 'John Pemberton', the Liverpool seaman who claimed that honour. His newly married wife, Emma J. Head, wrote to Consul Sprague on 31 July, 1873, on the official notepaper of J. W. Winchester and Company, requesting that he send the effects belonging to her husband to New York. Mr Sprague acknowledged her letter on 19 August, and referred to her husband as 'the late Steward of the brig *Mary Celeste*.'

The considerable correspondence between U.S. Consul Sprague and officials in Germany, written in 1875 and 1885, which is on file in the United States National Archives, indicate that three of the missing crew, Volkert and Boz Lorensen and Arian Martens, were natives of the small village of Utersum on the island of Föhr, one of the Friersian group. The Chief of the Parish, R. I. Lorenzen, writes on 7 February 1885 to say that the mother of the Lorensen brothers is still living 'and she does not cease to deplore the loss of her two sons.

The eldest of whom was married, his wife and daughter are still living here under poor circumstances. The younger brother was betrothed and his bride has married another seaman and also lives in this village.' The wife and children of Arian Martens, he says, 'are likewise living in Amrun (another island) in uneasy circumstances. His parents, father and mother are still living'. None of the effects of the brothers Lorensen had reached their families, says the Chief of the Parish, 'because one supposes that it was not worthwhile claiming them.'

The Chief of the Parish of Utersum states that the Lorensen brothers were his former schoolmates. Concerning A. Martens, Mr Lorenzen states that he had passed his mate's examination and 'was already navigating several years from Hamburg as such'. All three men, he declared, had enjoyed for their class as seamen 'an extraordinary good education which is generally the case in all our islands.' He concludes his letter with these words: 'that the same must have lost their lives, I take as a fact, but I cannot admit that they have had a share in any act of violence or in any mutiny which is guaranteed to me (by) the character of the men in question who were of a most peaceful disposition.' Mr Lorenzen enclosed a letter from Kunot Martens, father of Arian, who stated he had received a letter from his grandson in New York, written in 1884, which referred to the infamous lies and inventions about the Mary Celeste which had appeared in an English journal and had been reprinted in the newspaper *Echo*.

Of the fifth seaman, Gottlieb Goodschall, a young man of 23 whose name is variously spelt as 'Goodschaud' or 'Goodschaal' and who is described, like the other seamen, as having 'fair hair and light complexion,' no further details are available, beyond the fact that his country of birth is listed as 'Germany'. We may note here that in a letter written on 4 April 1873 Consul Sprague refers to three members of the *Mary Celeste's* crew. He wrote to the Department of State:

> I beg to enclose copy of a communication which I have this day received from Prussia, asking for information regarding some of the missing crew of the derelict *Mary Celeste*. It is somewhat gratifying to learn three out of the five men composing the crew of the *Mary Celeste* were known to the writer of that

> communication as being peaceful and first class sailors, as it further diminishes the probability that any violence was committed on board of this vessel by her crew.

Mr Fay points out that 'further evidence as to the character of the crew comes from the letter written by Captain Briggs two days before his vessel left her East River pier, wherein he states: "We seem to have a very good Mate and Steward", and four days later Mrs Briggs writes to her husband's mother "Benjamin thinks we have got a pretty peaceful set this time all around, if they continue as they have begun", adding, with characteristic Yankee caution, "can't tell yet how smart they are" '. Mr Fay observes 'There can be no question about the *Mary Celeste* being adequately manned. She carried a crew of 8, including the captain, and it seems reasonable to assume that Captain Briggs, experienced mariner that he was, would exercise more than ordinary care in the selection of a crew for a voyage on which his wife and two-year-old daughter were to accompany him.'

The presence on board of Captain Briggs, his wife and child, and the two mates, Albert Richardson and Andrew Gilling, and the characters they bore, are no less well attested.

Benjamin Spooner Briggs was born at Wareham, Mass., on 24 April, 1833, and was thus in 1872 thirty-seven years of age. He was the second of five sons born to Captain Nathan Briggs and his wife, Sophia Cobb. All but one of the boys, James, went to sea and all four became master mariners at an early age.

The life of the Briggs family has been described by Dr Oliver W. Cobb in his book *Rose Cottage*. As the nephew of Captain Nathan and the first cousin of both Benjamin Briggs and his wife Sarah, he knew the family intimately. Captain Nathan Briggs, he says, although kind and affectionate to his family, was a strict disciplinarian aboard ship. His sons were allowed to serve on his ships but:

> the etiquette of the sea ruled, and one would not have known but that they were strangers . . . He was a Spartan father when it came to having his sons on shipboard. They had to do the regular work of sailors, take their trick at the wheel, stand watch, help reef and furl sails. . . . The Captain expected his boy to be the first man aloft in an emergency. In addition to

this, the boy had regular lessons to study and to recite to the Captain; navigation, geography, history, literature. There was no idleness on these voyages.

When he was four years old, Benjamin and his mother went to live with her father, the Reverend Oliver Cobb, and he spent five years there while his father was at sea. But Captain Nathan set up home for his family again in 1844 at 'Rose Cottage' at Marion. Mr Fay says:

> It is not definitely known whether Benjamin, like his brothers, shipped under his father, but he was brought up in a home where a kindly discipline was maintained, and careful training in manners and deportment were considered essential. In the formation of his character, his mother, who it will be remembered was a minister's daughter, was always the powerful influence. The bond between them was unusually strong, and the last letter written by him, of which there is any record, was addressed to her in tender and affectionate terms, evincing solicitude for her comfort during his absence. This letter was sent just a few days prior to his sailing from New York.

On 9 September 1862, Benjamin Spooner Briggs, aged 27, and Sarah Elizabeth Cobb, aged 20, were married at Marion, Massachusetts, the ceremony being performed by the bride's father, the Reverend Leander Cobb, Pastor of the Congregational Church of Marion. 'Benjamin and Sarah had been boy and girl sweethearts. It was a love match, and they always remained deeply devoted to each other' states Dr Cobb. The certificate of the marriage, as also the birth certificates of the couple's two children, are printed by Mr Fay.

Benjamin and Sarah Briggs spent their honeymoon on a voyage to the Mediterranean, and they made several other voyages together in ships of which he was the Master. Their son, Arthur, was born on 20 September, 1865, and their daughter, Sophia Matilda, on 31 October, 1870.

Benjamin Briggs's reputation as a ship's Master was well established before he took command of the *Mary Celeste* and purchased a 8/24th interest in October 1872. He had previously commanded the schooner *Forest King*, the bark *Arthur* and the brig *Sea Foam*.

As his reputation has been tarnished by romancers and traducers it will not be out of place to repeat the words of Consul Horatio Jones Sprague who, writing from Gibraltar on 20 January 1873 to the Department of State at Washington, states that Captain Briggs 'was well known' and that 'he bore the highest character for seamanship and correctness'. Later, in a letter (3 April 1873) to N.W. Bingham, Treasury Department agent at Boston, Consul Sprague wrote: 'The missing master, Briggs, I had known for many years, and he always bore a good character as a Christian, and an intelligent and active shipmaster.' Consul Sprague, in his letter of 12 August 1873, to Mr James C. Briggs, brother of Captain Briggs, expressed sympathy and concluded with the statement: 'Your brother was well known to me and therefore I was able to appreciate his merits'.

Mr Charles Edey Fay, who acquired first hand information, says:

> Gentle and affectionate in his family relations, it seems reasonable to suppose that he would be just and considerate towards the men serving under him. He could be stern when occasion required it, and was not a man to be intimated or imposed upon. Born of sturdy, God-fearing New England stock; reared in an atmosphere of wholesome refinement; and trained as well in the salty curriculum of the sea as in the ways of right living, Benjamin Briggs was well prepared to undertake the responsibilities of the command of the *Mary Celeste*.

Of Sarah Elizabeth Cobb, who became Mrs Briggs, we know that she was fond of music and had a good voice. Dr Cobb recalls his father praising her after a Sunday morning service for the excellent quality of her singing. She is depicted as a practical New England housewife, a good mother and wife who, we know, had her harmonium and sewing machine shipped on board the *Mary Celeste*.

Albert G. Richardson, the *Mary Celeste's* first mate, was the son of Theodore W. Richardson, of Stockton Springs, Maine, and in the crew list signed on 4 November, 1872, he gave his age as 28. He had served as a private in the Maine Coast Guard in the war between the States, receiving an honourable discharge, a period of service which produced a pension for his widow. He had served on ships owned by Captain Winchester for two years and he married a niece of the *Mary Celeste's* principal owner, who, in an interview published in the *New York Sunday World* on 24 January 1886, describes him as a 'man of excellent character'. Richardson had also previously sailed under Captain Briggs, whose cousin, Dr Cobb, recalls hearing Captain Briggs congratulate Mrs Briggs upon their good fortune in having Richardson to go with them as first mate on the *Mary Celeste*.

Andrew Gilling, the second mate who gave his age as 25 in 1872, appears, from the letter previously quoted by the Pastor of his Parish, to have been a Dane, and that is all we know of him. Of the *Mary Celeste's* 'steward and cook' Edward William Head, who was aged 23, Captain Winchester stated in 1886, in the *New York Sunday World* 'The steward was a white man who belonged to Williamsburg where he was respected by all who knew him, and he had just been married when the brig sailed.'

Of Captain Winchester, the vessel's principal owner and agent, Mr Fay (who as a member of the firm which insured the ship had access to reliable records) says, in reference to the allegation of the gentleman in Gibraltar who suggested that Captain Winchester had 'hired the crew to make away with the officers', that 'the idea of Captain Winchester conspiring with the crew of the *Mary Celeste* to murder its officers was, indeed, ridiculous. Captain Winchester was well known and highly respected in maritime circles.' He died in 1912.

Mr Fay tells us, 'For years a warm friendship had existed between him and the Briggs family. Captain Nathan Briggs, father of Captain Benjamin, had commanded, from 1851 to 1853, the fine ship *Winchester*, owned by J.W. Winchester and Company'.

To complete the picture of the people who made up the *dramatis personnae* of the 'mystery' of the *Mary Celeste*, the following information has been collected by Mr Fay regarding the principal men on board the *Dei Gratia*. Captain David Reed Morehouse was born on 22 March, 1838, at Sandy Cove, Nova Scotia, and he went to sea at the age of 16, becoming a captain when he was 21. Mr Fay quotes a correspondent who wrote to him to say that Morehouse 'was admired by seafaring men for his knowledge of navigation', and an old resident of Bear Island, Nova Scotia, who stated, 'He was very honourable in his dealings and a good citizen.' The chief mate, Oliver Deveau, was born on 9 September, 1838, at Plympton,

Digby County, Nova Scotia. The *Digby Courier* of 20 September, 1912, writes:

Death of Captain Oliver E. Deveau

The last survivor of the Brigt. *Mary Celeste* mystery has passed away.

Captain Oliver E. Deveau died at his home in Brighton on Tuesday, the 10th instant, aged 76 years. The deceased was born at Cape St Marys' moving to Brighton when he was a young man. He was an old-time sailor, a thorough officer, and a man capable of sailing a ship to any part of the world. His last voyage was to Cuba some four or five years ago when he was obliged to leave his ship, owing to illness, and return home. He is survived by a widow, one son, James Deveau, who holds a responsible position with the telephone company in Springfield, Mass. and two daughters, Mrs Jessie M. Elanson, of Plymouth – Mass., and Miss Addie A., at home.

13

The *Mary Celeste* sails

Captain Briggs left his home in Marion, Massachusetts, on 19 October, 1872, to take command of the *Mary Celeste*, which had been brought to New York on 5 September from Cow Bay, Cape Breton, by Captain J.W.Spates on completion of a voyage from Porto Rico. The *Mary Celeste* berthed at New York first at Pier 44, East River, at Hunters Point and then at Pier 50, East River, from where she finally sailed for Genoa. On Sunday, 27 October Mrs Briggs, accompanied by her two-year-old daughter, arrived at the Fall River Line's North River Pier, where they were met by Captain Briggs, who conveyed them and their baggage across town to his ship. Their son, Arthur, was left with Grandmother Briggs to complete his schooling. The loading of the cargo of 1,700 barrels of alcohol was completed on 2 November, as we learn from the letter written by Captain Briggs to his mother next day (letter printed by Mr Fay by permission from Mr J.Franklin Briggs).

New York Nov. 3rd, 1872.

My Dear Mother,

It is a long time since I have written you a letter and I should like to give you a real interesting one but I hardly know what to say except that I am well and the rest of us ditto. It is such a long time since I composed other than business epistles. It seems to me to have been a great while since I left home but it is only little over two weeks but in that time my mind has been filled with business cares and I am again launched away into the busy whirl of business life from which I have so long been laid aside. For a few days it was tedious, perplexing, and very tiresome, but now I have got fairly settled down to it and it sits lightly and seems to run more smoothly and my appetite keeps good and I hope I shan't lose any flesh. It seems real home-like since Sarah and Sophia have got here and we enjoy our little quarters. On Thursday we had a call from Willie [Rev. William H. Cobb, brother of Mrs Briggs, and for many years librarian of Congregational House, Boston, Mass.] and his wife – took Sophia and went with them on a ride up to Central Park. Sophia behaved splendid and seemed to enjoy a ride as much as any of us. It is the only time they have been away from the vessel. On account of the Horse disease the horsecars have not been running on this side of the city so we have not been able to go and make calls as we were so far away from anyone to go on foot, and to hire a private carriage would have cost us at least $10.00, a trip which we didn't feel able to pay and we couldn't walk and carry Sophia a mile or two which we should have had to [do] to get to ferry for Iva [word unintelligible] or E-port [probably Elizabethport]. It has been very confining for S. but I hope when we return we can make up for it. We seem to have a very good Mate and Steward and I hope shall have a pleasant voyage. We both have missed Arthur and I believe I should have sent for him if I could have thought of a good place to stow him away. Sophia calls for him occasionally and wants to see him in the Album which by the way is a favourite book of hers. She knows your picture in both Albums and points and says Gamma Bis. She seems real smart – has got over the bad cold she had when she came and has a first rate appetite for hash and bread and butter. I think the voyage will do her lots of good. We enjoy our melodeon and have some good sings. I was in hopes Oli [Oliver E. Briggs, brother of Benjamin] might get in before I left but I'm afraid not now. We finished loading last night and shall leave on Tuesday morning if we don't get off tomorrow night, the Lord willing. Our vessel is in beautiful trim and I hope we shall have a fine passage, but as I have never been in her before can't say how she'll sail. Shall want you to write us in about 20 days to Genoa, care of Am. Consul and about 20 days after to Messina care of Am. Consul who will forward to us if we don't go there. I wrote James [James C. Briggs, another brother of Benjamin] to pay you for A's board and rent: if he forgets, call on him – also for any money that may be necessary for clothes. Please get Eben to see his skates are all right and the holes in his new thick boot heels.

I hope he'll keep well as I think if he does he'll be some help as well as company for you. Love to Hannah. Sophia calls Aunt Hannah often: I wish we had a picture so she could remember the countenance as well as name – hoping to be with you again early in the spring, with much love I am

Yrs. affly. *BENJ.*

(At the top of the fourth page appear the following words) 'Shall leave Tuesday morning.'

On Monday, 4 November, Captain Briggs went to the New York office of the United States Shipping Commissioner and signed the 'Articles of Agreement' and the 'List of Persons Composing the Crew' of the *Mary Celeste*. On the same day an Atlantic Mutual underwriter initialled the insurance for J.W. Winchester and Co. for $3,400 on the vessel's freight on charter from New York to Genoa, Italy, at the rate of 2½%.

The *Mary Celeste* left her dock at Pier 50 East River on Tuesday morning, 5 November, but, owing to unfavourable weather, anchored off Staten Island; from where, on 7 November, Mrs Briggs wrote to her husband's mother.

Dear Mother Briggs –

Probably you will be a little surprised to receive a letter with this date, but instead of proceeding to sea when we came out Tuesday morning, we anchored about a mile or so from the city, as it was a strong head wind, and B. [Benjamin] said it looked so thick & nasty ahead we shouldn't gain much if we were beating & banging about. Accordingly we took a fresh departure this morning with wind light but favorable, so we hope to get outside without being obliged to anchor. Have kept a sharp look-out for Oliver [Captain Oliver Everson Briggs, brother of Benjamin, who was to lose his life within a few weeks] but so far have seen nothing of him. It was rather trying to lay in sight of the city so long & think that most likely we had letters waiting for us there, and be unable to get them. However, we hope no great change has occurred since we did hear and shall look for a goodly supply when we reach G. [Genoa].

Sophy thinks the figure 3 & the letter G. on her blocks is the same thing so I saw her whispering to herself yesterday with the 3 block in her hand – Gam-gam-gamma. Benj. thinks we have got a pretty peaceable set this time all around if they continue as they have begun. Can't tell yet how smart they are. B. reports a good breeze now, says we are going along nicely.

I should like to be present at Mr Kingsbury's ordination next week. Hope the people will be united in him, and wish we might hear of Mrs K's improved health on arrival. Tell Arthur I make great dependence on the letter I shall get from him, and will try to remember anything that happens on the voyage which he would be pleased to hear.

We had some baked apples (sour) the other night about the size of a new-born infant's head. They tasted extremely well.

Please give our love to Mother & the girls, Aunt Hannah, Arthur and other friends, reserving a share for yourself.

As I have nothing more to say I will follow A. Ward's advice, and say it at once.

Farewell, Yours aff'ly, *SARAH*

On Thursday morning, 7 November, the *Mary Celeste* left her Staten Island anchorage to start her memorable voyage 'with wind light but favourable' as Mrs Briggs recorded. 'A voyage', observes Mr Fay, 'destined to lift her from comparative obscurity to a place of enduring fame in the chronicles of the sea.'

Meanwhile the *Dei Gratia* had been loading her cargo of petroleum at New York, the consignees being Simpson and Shaw. On 30 October she was docked in the Eerie Basin, while the *Mary Celeste* was at Pier 50, East River, the *Dei Gratia* moving on 6 November to Venango Yard. She sailed from New York on 15 November, eight days *after* the *Mary Celeste*, on a voyage to Gibraltar where she was to await orders. These details are of some importance, and they are taken from the *New York Journal of Commerce*, and the *Maritime Register*, because it has been stated that the two ships which were to meet so dramatically in mid-ocean on 5 December, lay alongside each other in New York and that the *Dei Gratia* sailed first.

In Chapter I of this book it is stated that Captain Briggs and Morehouse dined together in New York on the night before the *Mary Celeste* sailed. This is stated on the authority of a letter written by Mrs Morehouse to Mr J. G. Lockhart, who mentions it in his book, published in 1927.

The *Dei Gratia* followed a more northerly course than the *Mary Celeste*, passed to the north of the Azores and she was spoken to by another ship at Latitude 40°.55'N and Longitude 66W on 19 November. Her course for Gibraltar was S.E. by E. and throughout her voyage her log records that the wind blew from the North West,

North and North East, from which quarter it came on 5 December, the day she met up with the derelict when, for the first time in her voyage, the log records any fact other than course and wind. On that day the log of the *Dei Gratia* states:

> Course S.E. ½ E. wind N.N.E. Begins with fresh breeze and clear, sea still running heavy but wind moderating. Saw a sail to the E. 2 p.m. saw she was under very short canvas steering very wild and evidently in distress. Hauled up to speak to her and render assistance if necessary. At 3 p.m. hailed her and getting no answer and seeing no one on deck (got) out boat and sent mate and 2 men on board, sea running high at the time. He boarded her without accident and returned in about an hour and reported her to be the *Mary Celeste* of and from New York for Genoa abandoned with 3½ feet of water in the hold.

14

The testimony

The evidence given in the Vice-Admiralty Court at Gibraltar in 1872 and 1873 records the only known facts about the finding of the *Mary Celeste* and her condition on 5 December. This evidence is supplemented by the various reports and surveys commissioned by Mr Solly Flood, the Queen's Proctor.

These documents, the true dossier of the drifting derelict, correct the mis-statements which have been made about the vessel's condition and what was found on her by Mate Deveau and his men. They disclose that there was no half-eaten breakfast on the cabin table, no cups of tea still warm to the touch, no cat sleeping peacefully on a locker, and, most important of all, no boats. The evidence of Oliver Deveau, Chief Mate of the *Dei Gratia*, and his men, shatters the fable that when they boarded her, the *Mary Celeste's* boats were hanging from their davits or lying in chocks on the main hatch. For nearly eighty years, since Conan Doyle stated the boats were intact, legions of amateur detectives have sought to discover the means by which Captain Briggs and his companions left the vessel. The answer is obvious; they left in the ship's boat. Why they did so is a question we shall need to consider later.

No secret was made in 1873 of the fact that the *Mary Celeste's* boats were missing. The *New York Journal of Commerce* stated on 11 January. 'There were no boats on board when she was found' and this statement was repeated exactly by the *Maritime Register* four days later. Both Captain Coffin (*New York World* 24 January

1886) and Allan Kelly (*New York Evening Post* 15 October 1904) told their readers that the ship's boat was gone. The evidence given in the Vice-Admiralty Court at Gibraltar goes far further than that. It provides the only reliable information upon which a likely solution of the mystery can be based.

The facts ascertained at the Salvage Enquiry can be arranged under several headings.

THE SIGHTING OF THE DERELICT

Captain Morehouse stated that when he came on deck about 1 p.m. on 5 December, he saw a sail on the weather bow bearing East-North-East, and steering West-South-West, the wind was North-North-East, and the *Dei Gratia* was steering South-East-Half-East. His ship was on the port tack and the strange vessel, which he judged to be about six miles distant, was on the starboard tack. He watched her through his glass and, due to the little sail she carried, he judged that there was something amiss, and he bore up towards her. Some fifteen minutes later he saw the vessel yawing and he noticed what he thought was a flag of distress flying at her yard (which he learned subsequently was the flapping sail). In reply to the judge's question, Captain Morehouse said:

> I think the jib was trimmed on the port side when we first met her although she was on the opposite tack. I have seen vessels behave so strangely that it is impossible to say how or what they will do. She was yawing coming into the wind and then falling off again. I watched her for two hours doing that.

He thought, he said, that it was possible that the vessel might have been further to the East before he first sighted her, and he gave his opinion that she had worn round. The fact that her yards were square led him to believe that when she was abandoned, she was running before the wind. It was possible, he thought, that the storm from the North-North-East he had met in his own vessel at 4 o'clock that morning might have sent her round, had she also met it.

The *Dei Gratia* came alongside the vessel, about 300 or 400 yards off, about 3 p.m., he told the Court. They hailed her but got no answer and they saw no one on the decks. Second Mate Wright said there was a tolerably heavy sea running when he and Deveau rowed to the vessel.

The testimony given by Oliver Deveau, First Mate of the *Dei Gratia*, about the sighting of the vessel does something to help in the final analysis. He stated:

> Her head was westward when we first saw her. She was on starboard tack. With her foresails set she would come up to the wind and fall off again. The wind was North, not much then, though blowing heavily in the morning. With the sails she had set when I first saw her, she might come up and fall away a little but not much. She would always keep those sails full. The sheet was fast on the port side. She was found on starboard tack.

Deveau and Wright boarded the *Mary Celeste*, while Seaman Johnson held the boat at her side. On his second trip, when he took charge of the derelict, Deveau was accompanied by Seamen Charles Lund and Augustus Anderson. Deveau said his first act was to sound the pumps with the sounding rod which was lying on the deck; he found 3½ feet of water and there was a great deal of water below decks.

CABIN

Everything in the main cabin, which was slightly raised above the deck, was wet. Its door was open and its skylight raised. The windows on the starboard side were nailed up with planks and canvas, and those on the port side were shut. Deveau found charts, books and the log-slate, which had been entered up to 25 November and showed the vessel had made the island of St Mary, lying on the table. In the mate's cabin he found the Log Book which had been entered up to 24 November, and a chart showing the vessel's track to that date. Everything, he said, seemed to have been left behind in a great hurry. He judged from various articles of female clothing there had been a woman aboard, and an imprint on the bed gave him the impression that a child had lain on it. He saw articles of a child's wearing apparel, and toys, scattered about. The bed was wet. It had been slept in and was not made. The rack (the 'fiddle' used to prevent dishes sliding off) was in position on the table but there were no eatables. There was nothing in the cabin to eat or drink. The wetness of everything in the cabin, he attributed to the rain coming in from a squall that morning. There was no phial of oil, no bottle of cough mixture, we note.

In the cabin Deveau found two boxes of clothing, of the usual sort worn by men and women, a work bag containing needles, threads and buttons, various books of a religious nature, a case of instruments, a writing desk, a dressing case, a bag of dirty clothes, a pair of sea boots, a clock which had stopped (but he didn't mention the time it showed), a sewing machine under the sofa, and a rosewood melodium or harmonium beneath the skylight. There was no chronometer, sextant, or Navigation Book, and the ship's papers and Register were missing. Under the Captain's berth he discovered subsequently a sword. He took it out and looked at it. He drew it from its sheath. 'There was nothing remarkable on it. I did not think there is anything remarkable about it,' he told the Court. Shown the sword, he agreed it now seemed rusty. He put it back where he found it, he stated.

Deveau's evidence about the sword brought the observation from Mr Solly Flood that it had been cleaned with lemon which had covered it with a citrate of iron thus destroying the marks of the supposed blood which, therefore, was not blood at all, as was at first supposed, but another substance put there to destroy and disguise the original marks of blood which were once there. Mr Flood was clearly loath to give up without a struggle his best evidence for his theory of mutiny and murder.

Deveau's discoveries in the cabin were corroborated by Seaman Lund, who stated, 'I did not see any bread or food', and by Wright, who said, 'I did not see anything in the cabin more than in any other cabin'. He saw nothing particular there to call his attention, he stated.

Deveau, we may remark, did not mention finding the words 'Fanny, My Dear Wife. Frances N.R.' scratched on the log-slate, but in his evidence at Gibraltar Captain Winchester stated he saw these words on the slate, which he took to be the start of a message scribbled by Mate Richardson to his wife. Mrs Richardson, we recall, said in 1902 they were so found.

THE GALLEY

Deveau and Wright next examined the galley, which they found with its door open and a foot deep in water. The sea appeared to have come in. The stove was knocked out of place and the cooking utensils were scattered about.

THE FORECASTLE

Deveau said he found the seamen's oilskins, boots and even their pipes scattered about as if they had left in great haste.

DECK

They found the mainhatch fastened down and the forehatch and the hatch of the lazaret (the space in the after part of the vessel where provisions and spare gear were stowed) both off. Deveau did not say that the forehatch was bottom up. There were plenty of provisions, enough for six months and the casks were in their proper place, but the water casks on deck had been moved, as if by a heavy sea. The binnacle was stove in, its compass destroyed. The wheel was not lashed.

MARKS ON RAIL AND BLOODSTAINS

Deveau stated:

> I did not notice any mark of an axe on the rail or cut. I did not see this cut in the rail now shown me to notice it. I cannot say how the cut came in the rail. It appears to have been done with a sharp axe and I do not think it would have been done by my men whilst we were in possession of the vessel. I did not see any new axes on board the *Celeste*. There was an old axe we found on board. I can form no opinion about the cause of the axe cut on the rail. I noticed no marks or traces of blood upon the deck. I cannot say whether there were any or not. We never washed the decks of the *Mary Celeste* nor scraped them. We had not men enough for that. The sea washed over the decks. [The Queen's Proctor explained that salt water contains chloric acid which dissolves particles of the blood.] If there are some parts of the deck or sail scraped I did not notice them and they were not done whilst we were on board.

In respect to the marks on the rail, Captain Winchester stated they were not there when the vessel sailed from New York. He had never seen the sword shown him in Captain Brigg's possession, he said. His comment on the religious books found in the Captain's cabin was that he would expect them to be there as Captain Briggs was a teetotaller and a religious man.

VESSEL AND CARGO

The masts were in good condition and the hull appeared to be new, stated Deveau. The general condition of the ship was sea-worthy. The cargo of alcohol was in good condition, well stowed and had not shifted. It was not injured. He found, he said, no wine, beer or spirits in the ship. Captain Winchester, in his testimony, said he saw the cargo of 1,701 barrels of alcohol put on board. Beneath it were 30 tons of stone ballast. To his knowledge the ship carried no other cargo. The ship, he said, was chartered by Meissner, Ackerman and Company, merchants of New York, a very respectable German firm known to him personally. Wright said he found the anchors and chains on board, there being nothing to show that the vessel had been moored and had then parted her cable.

BOATS

Deveau stated:

> There were no boats and no davits at the side. I don't think she used davits. It appeared as if she carried her boat on deck; there was a spar lashed across the stern davits so that no boat had been there. There were no spare spars on the decks of the *Mary Celeste* whatever. When there is no boat on the davits in the stern, there is often a spar lashed to keep the davits steady. In this case the spar was lashed thro' the sheave holes [the spaces between the cheeks of a block] which showed there had been no boat there. The *Celeste* had not accommodation on deck for two boats. One could see where the boat had been lashed across the main hatch, but that was not the right place for her. There were no lashings visible: therefore I cannot swear that the *Mary Celeste* had any boat at all, but there were two fenders where the boat would be lashed. Assuming that there was a boat, there was nothing to show how the boat was launched. There were no signs of any tackles to launch her. We

launched our boat that way from the rail of the vessel without tackle or hoisting her up, with a tow rope only to secure her.

Deveau was questioned again about the boats after he had been brought back from Genoa. He then said:

When I went on board I found the rails on both sides lying on the deck lashed or fastened at one end. I cannot say whether my men replaced them with lashings or took off the lashing from the ends of the rails that were lashed. The rail fits in tight in the socket and it takes some force to remove or raise it and also to replace it. The lashing was a temporary rope and the lashing not a regular tight lashing. There was the appearance of one boat having been on board. I could not see any means or tackle for hoisting the boat on or off deck and therefore conclude the boat must have been launched. I saw no remains or pieces of a painter or boat's rope fastened to the rail.

Wright and Lund were both questioned about the boats. Wright, in reply to Mr Solly Flood, said:

There were davits to hang a boat to astern. They were in good state. I could not tell one way or the other whether a boat had been launched from them. I could not tell whether any boat had or had not been there at all. There were no davits on the quarter of the vessel. I saw nothing from which I could judge whether a boat had been upon deck. I saw no lashings out loose. I saw no ropes on either side showing that a boat had been launched from the ship at all. I observed no remains of any tow line.

Lund saw no boats on board. He concluded from the fixings on the main hatch that a boat had been lashed there.

Captain Marcus H. Tracey, who was at Gibraltar early in 1873, informed Mr Fay in 1930 that he was told by Captain Winchester that the owners, when they learned that Captain Briggs was taking his wife and child on the voyage, put an additional boat on board which was placed on a cradle over the main hatch but, prior to the ship's departure, one of her boats had been damaged during the loading of the cargo.

SAILS AND RIGGING

The exact state of the sails and rigging, as they were observed on 5 December, are an important guide to the abandonment of the vessel.

Deveau said that the rigging was in very bad order but the standing rigging was all right. The upper foretopsail and foretopsail were gone, apparently blown from the yards. The lower foretopsail was hanging by its four corners. The mainsail was hauled down and it was lying loose, as if it had been run down, on the forward hatch. The jib and foretopsail were set. All the other sails were furled. He explained further:

> The topgallant masts and topmasts were all up. She had four yards, two topgallant and fore yards and topgallant royal yards. The royal and topgallant sails were furled and the running rigging of those sails was all in proper place. The rigging out of order was forebraces on port side, broken; starboard lower topsail brace broken, main peak halyards broken, the gear of the foresail all broken clewlings, and buntings gone.

When he was recalled to give further evidence, Deveau gave these answers:

> I have stated that I found the peak halyard on the *Mary Celeste* broken when I went on board. I had a fresh rope put in its place, but not a new rope, and that will account for the Surveyors not finding the rope spliced or mended. I can not say how the halyard had been broken. It was a very old one and had been spliced.
>
> When the wind is right dead aft we often do not carry a mainsail though sometimes it may be. Looking at the Log of the *Mary Celeste*, as now shown me, the wind appears to have been aft and therefore would not require the mainsail to be set.
>
> There is an entry in the Log of the mainsail having been again set.

Seaman Lund, we need to note, stated, 'The peak halyards were broken and gone', and Seaman Anderson said there were ropes and all kinds of running gear, sheets and braces, hanging over both sides of the vessel.

THE WEATHER

Both Captain Morehouse and Mate Deveau stated that the weather during the days before they found the *Mary Celeste* had been stormy and the wind was North-Westerly. Morehouse told the Court, 'The weather had been blowing very hard for seven or eight days previous but had on that morning commenced to moderate.'

THEORIES OF ABANDONMENT

Invited to give the Court his theory why the people of the *Mary Celeste* left their vessel, Deveau answered:

> It did not occur to me that there had been any act of violence. There was nothing whatever to induce one to believe or to show that there had been any violence.
>
> I used often when at the wheel to think how and why the the vessel had been abandoned by her crew and came to the conclusion that she had been left in panic, that being also strengthened by the sounding rod found near the pump and her sails being rather injured.
>
> She was so sound and stout that I cannot think that if I had been on board I should have abandoned her. I should have considered her safer than an open boat unless she was on the rocks.
>
> My idea is that the crew got alarmed, and, by the sounding rod being found lying alongside the pumps, that they had sounded the pumps and found perhaps a quantity of water in the pumps at the moment and, thinking she would go down, abandoned her. The pumps would be sounded perhaps every two hours or four hours. In order to make entry in the Log of 'pumps carefully attended to' the pumps should be sounded every watch or every four hours. If the vessel were leaky more often. The fact of finding the vessel with only four feet of water when I boarded her shows that she made little or no water, about one inch in twenty-four hours, and therefore I conclude that all the water found in her went down her hatches and through the cabin.

Asked by the judge to explain his theory further, Deveau replied:

> The only explanation of the abandonment which I can give is that there was a panic from the belief that the vessel had more water in her than she had as afterwards proved. I cannot

> give an opinion as to whether the derelict could have run the distance where we found her in the interval with the sails she had set. She was going steadily from 1½ to 2 knots when we saw her, with the wind on her beam. She might have had more sails set at first. She would not run steadily before the wind with her rudder unlashed. She had two headsails set, jib and foretop-staysail set on the starboard tack. Her yards were square, her lower foretopsail was hanging by the four corners, the wind was to the Northward, her head to the Westward. She was then going in opposite direction to ourselves. We met her. She probably had changed her course more than once. She was going backwards. It is impossible to say therefore how long or how often she had changed her course.

Upon being asked the same question, Captain James Winchester had this to say:

> Captain Briggs bore a high character, the character of a courageous officer and good seaman who would not, I think, desert his ship except to save his life. I also knew the Mate Richardson. I had done so for two years. He was an experienced and courageous officer in whom I had great confidence. I believe he had presence of mind. His three previous Captains spoke of him as fit to command any ship and I believe he would not leave his ship except for life or death. From what I have seen of the state and condition of the vessel I cannot believe that she was abandoned by her Master, Officers and Crew in consequence of stress of weather only. I had plenty of time to examine her thoroughly and feel very certain that she was not abandoned through perils of sea.

He was very certain, he said, that, 'both men would remain by their ship to the last and that neither would have deserted the ship unless forced to do so for fear of their lives.'

VOYAGE TO GIBRALTAR

As allegations have been made that something suspicious occurred on the *Mary Celeste* before she reached Gibraltar, it may be as well to state that Deveau testified that the *Mary Celeste*, on approaching the Straits, was swept past Gibraltar and along the Spanish coast 30 to 40 miles to the East. He got back to Gibraltar on 13 December, on the morning after the *Dei Gratia* had made that port.

THE AWARD FOR SALVAGE

The smallness of the award, £1,700, has been taken to suggest that the Court was suspicious of the claim made by Captain Morehouse. He and his men expected to receive one-half of the total value of vessel and cargo. They were given only a fifth. On their behalf, their advocate stressed the risks they had run in bringing in the derelict, which left their own ship short-handed. The *Mary Celeste*, he remarked, had been found abandoned with her hatches open in mid-ocean at the stormiest time of year. But the judge did not choose to be generous. That may have been due to his annoyance that Deveau had been allowed to leave the jurisdiction of the Court before completing his evidence, or it may have resulted from the suspicions of Mr Solly Flood that there had been foul play and that the missing crew might still turn up, a belief he held until the end of his life.

15

Inventory

To complete the record of facts relating to the *Mary Celeste*, as disclosed at Gibraltar, there are the reports of the Surveyor of Shipping and the analysis of her timbers and of the sword blade made by Doctor Patron to consider. As well as these documents, some useful information may be derived from the Inventory of Articles found on board, made by Consul Sprague and the new master, Captain Blatchford, which was sent to the Department of State in Washington. The gist of these reports has already been given, and as they may be of interest to enquiring readers, their full texts are printed in the Appendix, it being necessary here to remark only that the marks on the vessel's bows were the only trace of unusual injury Mr Austin found.

There were no signs that the *Mary Celeste* had suffered from heavy seas and none to suggest that an explosion or fire had occurred, or the slightest trace of anything calculated to create alarm of fire or an explosion. Five hours' meticulous examination by an expert failed to present any reason *why* the vessel might have been abandoned in mid-ocean.

The affidavit sworn on oath by Ricardo Portunato, diver, being of a negative nature, does not require detailed consideration. The purpose of his inspection of the ship's hull, below the water-line, was, he says, to ascertain 'if possible whether she had sustained any damage or injury from a collision or from having struck upon any rock or shoal or otherwise howsoever.' The hull, stern keel, stern post and rudder did not, he reports, exhibit 'any trace of damage or injury' and 'they were in thoroughly good order and condition.' If the vessel had met with accident or casualty, he would have been able to discover it, reported Ricardo Portunato.

As some readers may have seen the article written by Mr Harold T. Wilkins, *Light on the Mystery of the 'Mary Celeste'* which appeared in the *Quarterly Review*, July, 1931, it is necessary to comment on his query, regarding the supposed blood stains on the sword. 'Why did Sir James Cockrane censure Deveau for "doing away with the vessel which had rendered necessary the analysis of the supposed blood stains"?' Elsewhere in the article, Mr Wilkins asks 'Why, also, should the mate of the *Dei Gratia*, Oliver Deveau, twice have destroyed important evidence found on the *Mary Celeste*? He made away with the mysterious "vessel", for which he was severely censured by the British judge; and evidently he cleaned with lemon the supposed blood marks on the picturesque and unusual type of sword in its scabbard found on the floor of the captain's cabin.' Mr Wilkins observes, 'These do not look like the unthinking actions of a seaman innocent and totally ignorant of the requirements of courts of law and justice', and he asked, 'What were his motives in so destroying evidence?'

Mr Wilkins, whose article is singularly free from the usual inaccuracies, clearly supports the theory of violence. In the hands of a skilful cross-examiner at the Old Bailey, the mate of the *Dei Gratia* might have been forced to tell the truth, he suggests, and thereby put the police on the track of the criminals who made away with the captain, his family and crew of the *Mary Celeste*. In support of this theory, which apparently puts the blame on the men of the *Dei Gratia*, Mr Wilkins quotes a letter written to him by the only surviving sister of mate Albert Richardson of the *Mary Celeste* in which she declares, 'The mystery will never be solved, as the only people who could throw any light on the tragedy are the crew of the *Dei Gratia*, and they have long since disappeared'. 'Did it ever occur to you that they were responsible?' she asks Mr Wilkins. 'The crew of the *Mary Celeste* were foully murdered' asserted Mrs Priscilla Richardson Shelton. Her late brother, Captain Lyman Richardson, agreed with her. 'By some means, they were decoyed to the other vessel, or part of them, then the extermination of the rest was easy as they carried no firearms for protection.' She told Mr Wilkins she was firmly convinced that was the true solution to the mystery, a theory which is seriously jeopardized by her incorrect statement that the *Dei Gratia* sailed from New York ten days before the *Mary Celeste* and was waiting for her.

Mr Wilkins's reference to the judge's censure of Mate Deveau for doing away with the mysterious vessel, meaning some 'container', which had rendered necessary the analysis of the supposed blood-stains, is derived, not from the transcript of evidence, in which it does not appear, but from the comment attributed to the judge by the *Gibraltar Chronicle and Commercial Intelligencer* on 24 March (quoted in Chapter 111) which appears to have mis-quoted Sir James Cockrane who, we see from the transcript of evidence, criticised the salvors only for 'going away' in their vessel before the inquiry had been completed, with the result that Deveau was brought back from Genoa.

Mr Wilkins's claim that Deveau had evidently destroyed some mysterious 'vessels or container' is repeated in the chapter devoted to the *Mary Celeste* in that author's book, *Mysteries Solved and Unsolved*, 1958.

Finally, there is the Inventory of Articles found on board the derelict *Mary Celeste*. This need not be considered in detail but certain items require to be noted:

> A doll, a harmoniphon (the harmonium), a child's high chair, a pocket-book containing $1 in Spanish Gold coin, $1 in American Silver coin, 25 cents in American coppers, a pair of cloth pants with suspenders, a silver watch, two pairs of child's shoes, two music books, a sword, a log book, a sewing machine, a silk umbrella, a basket of needles, a parasol, a box of child's toys, child's dresses and coat, a chest marked 'Arian Martens' (containing, amongst other things, a sextant and a flute), a desk (supposed to belong to Captain Briggs) containing account books, letters and receipts from J. W. Winchester and Company amounting to $3,600 and all dated in October 1872 (representing presumably the purchase price of his share in the *Mary Celeste*).

The items respecting a child and 'Arian Martens' confirm the presence on board of Sophia Matilda Briggs, aged two years (which

Mr Lawrence Keating denies) and of a seaman of that name (which Mr Keating also denies). That the seaman's chest contained a sextant corroborates the membership of the crew of a man of that name for, we recall, the Chief of the Parish of Utersum states that Arian Martens 'had passed his Mate's examination and was already navigating several years from Hamburg as such.'

As well as these items, a quantity of men's and women's clothes were found in the cabin, and of seamen's clothes and possessions in the forecastle. Captain Brigg's 'cloth pants with suspenders' (i.e. to the British 'trousers' and 'braces') is specifically mentioned because their presence on board has been taken to emphasise the hurry in which the master abandoned his vessel, presumably 'trouserless'.

This point was particularly emphasised by Mr Solly Flood in a letter to Consul Sprague in 1885, which shows that he still held the theory he had first advanced in 1872. He said the vessel 'had been wantonly disfigured and damaged for the obvious but ill-disguised purpose of making her appear to have been abandoned as unseaworthy', and he referred to one of the barrels of alcohol as having been 'tampered with'. Continuing his recital of the state in which the vessel was found, he remarks 'a few and inconsiderable marks of violence were found on deck, but as the evidence proved the crew to have been in possession of the vessel for some time longer than the Master, the Chief Mate, and, as I expect, the Second Mate, they had ample opportunity to remove appearances of violence had there been any'. He had, he said, spared no pains to discover the fate of the ten persons who had been on board and to discover what, if any, serious crime, and by whom, had been committed 'besides that of disfiguring and casting away the vessel on board her or after abandonment', and he referred to the necessity there was to enquire into what violence had been committed, 'as there was too much reason to fear.'

Commenting on Solly Flood's views, in a letter to the Secretary of State, Consul Sprague stated confidentially, 'Mr Flood is an Irish gentleman. Although reported as being over eighty years of age, has always been considered an individual of very vivid imagination, and to have survived, to some extent at least, the judicious application of his mental faculties; such is, I believe, the general opinion of the community at large, even among his most intimate and personal friends.' With this letter, Sprague forwarded to Washington, the joint opinion of Advocates Martin W. Stokes and George F. Cornwell, who had represented the parties in the salvage claim, which was to the effect that:

> The *Mary Celeste* had evidently met with very bad weather and appeared to have been left by the crew in a moment of sudden panic. There was not the slightest appearance of anything criminal having occurred. The Boat in which the crew had left her had not been hoisted up by Tackles but forced over the side of the Vessel. The Boat and crew had never been heard of since and there can be no doubt that in attempting to reach land, probably the Azores, the boat was swamped.

The information contained in the testimony given in the Vice-Admiralty Court and these documents will be considered in the next chapter in which we shall attempt to find a solution to the mystery of the famous drifting derelict.

16

The solution to the mystery

'No story of the sea has ever perplexed and fascinated men so strangely as the affair of the *Mary Celeste*. There is something about that conundrum of an empty ship, found in mid-ocean, with not a soul aboard and not a clue to explain what mischance had befallen her, which has never failed to draw to itself alike lovers of the sea and lovers of mysteries'. So wrote Mr. Lockhart in 1927.

In the ninety years which have elapsed since the *Mary Celeste* was brought into Gibraltar, a voluminous literature has grown up around her, 'much of it inspired rather by a craving for sensation rather than by a regard for historical accuracy', as Mr Lockhart observes, but it is, he points out, at least a witness to 'the abiding interest of the problem'. The puzzle of the drifting derelict has exercised the imagination of three generations of men and women and it has presented an irresistible temptation to romancers. Their repetitions and solutions have succeeded in surrounding the story with a cloud of imaginery circumstances which obscured the true facts and made the mystery insoluble, he remarks.

Mr Solly Flood gave the first kick to the ball of myth and mystery. He bruited his theory of foul play about the world, although his chief clue, the supposed blood stains on the sword, was demolished at once. His belief that one barrel of alcohol had been opened was unsubstantiated by any one else. He ignored the obvious solution – that the abandoned vessel's people had left in their own boat, of their own accord – and he preferred to think that the mutinous crew had escaped and were lurking about the world. Conan Doyle took it from there. He created a mystery which Sherlock Holmes himself couldn't have solved, for he established a situation which could be explained only by wild guesses. The ship's company had been wafted away by some outside agency, the amateur detectives decided. But when? Shortly before the *Dei Gratia* sighted her, they thought. The spark of imagination lighted the galley stove and laid a half-eaten breakfast on the cabin table. That was not enough for the myth-makers. As the legend progressed, the 'credo' became established. It was so firmly entrenched that neither Mr Lockhart's balanced survey or Mr Fay's researches could shatter it, for as late as 1954, we find Mr Dudley Pope, who contributed an article on the famous mystery to the London *Evening News* on 3 August stating there had been a long-stern chase, that a half-eaten meal lay on the cabin table and the seamen's mythical razors were 'bright and sharp'. But something had been achieved, for he extinguished the brightly burning galley fire and he acknowledged the vessel's boat was missing.

Whether the Great Myth is dead and buried remains to be seen. But there are still many questions to engage our attention. We need to ask ourselves three questions: does any suspicion attach to the *Mary Celeste's* crew? Did all ten people who comprised the ship's company leave in the boat? Does any suspicion surround the captain and crew of the *Dei Gratia*?

Mr Solly Flood, the imaginative and over-eager Queen's Proctor believed that the derelict's crew, inflamed by alcohol, had murdered their officers and, some days later, escaped on another ship. Mrs Priscilla Richardson Shelton, the mate's sister, declared that her brother and his shipmates had been foully murdered by the men of the *Dei Gratia*. Other writers have suggested that the whole thing was a 'put up job', a case of collusion between the men of the two ships.

There are many objections to Mr Flood's theory of foul play. Commercial alcohol is undrinkable and there was no other drink on board; the crew had no motive for mutiny. They were respectable men and it is inconceivable that they murdered their captain, his family and their officers and then departed in the boat in which they perished. Mrs Shelton's theory is equally unrewarding, especially as it was based on her untrue belief that the *Dei Gratia* preceded the *Mary Celeste* from New York.

The absence of the boat makes it certain that the captain, his wife, child and crew, or, if we are still in doubt about the conduct of the crew, some of them, left the *Mary Celeste* of their own free will. Why they deserted their staunch and sound vessel is a question to which we shall return. It seems equally certain that those who were in the boat perished at sea or on the rocky cliffs of St Mary for they were never heard of again.

The fact that the derelict was found sailing on her exact course ten days after the date of her probable abandonment does on the face of it seem suspicious, and it is claimed as an extraordinary and almost unbelieveable coincidence that she was found apparently abandoned in the wastes of the Atlantic by a brig from the same port, bound for the same port of call, whose captain is reputed to have been a friend of Benjamin Briggs.

A layman looking at a chart of the Atlantic cannot fail to notice that the currents between the Azores and the coasts of Portugal and Spain flow southward, and the wind, we are told by Morehouse and Deveau, at that time was generally from the north. Surely these combinations of wind and current would have swept the derelict far to the southward?

That is exactly what happened to the hulk *Julia*, a bark bound from London to Montreal which was abandoned on 4 December by her crew, who were brought into Holyhead, and which, according to *Lloyd's List*, was spoken to on 7 December at latitude 48 North and longitude 20 West. On the 13th the drifting hulk was sighted by S.S. *Olinda* at latitude 48 North and longitude 15 West, and on the 23rd she was noticed even further to the southward by the S.S. *Great Britain*, and it ended up in the Canary Islands. A glance at the chart will show that the *Julia* was abandoned not far from the course followed by the *Mary Celeste* and that she drifted progressively south. Why, therefore, did not the abandoned *Mary Celeste* do the same? Was it because she was still manned, as Mr Flood surmised?

Between the *Julia* and the *Mary Celeste* lay one great difference. The *Julia* was a dismasted hulk, the *Mary Celeste* a two-masted ship, with some sails set on her yards. The natural tendency is, a distinguished Admiral who first went to sea in 1899 tells me, for a sailing ship, under some sail, to hold up into the wind and not to drift with wind and current. That is what apparently happened with the *Mary Celeste* – an explanation which is supported by the testimony of Mate Deveau and Captain Morehouse. Deveau said that when she was sighted the *Mary Celeste* had her jib and fore-topsail set, the lower fore-topsail was hanging by its corners and two other sails, the upper fore-topsail and foresail, had been blown away. All the other sails lay loose on the deck or were furled. Her remaining sails were set on the starboard tack, though the vessel was on the port tack. As we have already seen, Deveau stated that the derelict was sailing westwards, in the opposite direction to her natural course, and the wind was north. He told the Court, 'With the sails she had set, she might come up and fall away a little, but not much. She would always keep those sails full.' Captain Morehouse, who watched the strange vessel through his telescope, for two hours, said 'She was yawing, coming into the wind and then falling off again', and he gave his opinion that 'the vessel had worn round before I picked her up. By the yards being square, I should say that when she was abandoned she was running before the wind'. He could not give any opinion, he said, as to whether she had been further to the east when he sighted her or whether the squall from the N.N.E., which the *Dei Gratia* had met at 4 o'clock that morning 'would have been likely to have sent her round, had she also met it'.

Dr Oliver Cobb gave the question of the *Mary Celeste*'s course, after abandonment, considerable thought. He worked out that by the time she was first sighted by the *Dei Gratia* at about 1.30 p.m. on 5 December, from the time of her last slate-log entry on 25 November at 8.0 a.m. she had covered more than 378½ miles because she must have sailed further eastwards before she turned round. When she was sighted she was making about 1½ to 2 knots, at which speed she could have sailed between 36 and 48 nautical miles a day. From the time of the log-slate entry it was nine-and-a-half days, and it was not difficult to work out that, if she had maintained this speed, she would have travelled between 333 and 444 miles. But she must have travelled further than that because, when she was abandoned on 25 November, five sails were set, which would have given her a higher average speed during the earlier part of her lone voyage.

Dr Cobb – whom Mr Charles Edey Fay describes as an experienced seaman who in his youth had sailed 'before the mast' and who became general manager of the Davis Coast Wrecking Company of New York, his activities taking him to South American, West Indian and American coastal waters – presented his theory to Mr Fay in a letter written on 10 May, 1941. He suggested:

> As the vessel sailed away after the change of wind which is reported to have come about this time (and being headed easterly with a northerly wind), there were three sails drawing, foresail, lower topsail and upper topsail. The foretopmast staysail and jib, being set on the port side, would not be of much use except as they would tend to prevent the vessel from coming into the wind and so keep her more steadily on her course. From 25 November to 5 December, northerly winds prevailed. The speed would be 3 to 4 miles per hour with ordinary winds, but the course sailed would be far from straight. She probably went easterly at about 2½ miles an hour, or, say 60 miles per 24 hours, for nearly eight days – or 480 miles. Then came a sudden change of wind – a squall perhaps. She came into the wind – shipped a sea (which accounted for the water in the galley and most of that in the hold, as the fore hatch was off) – lost her foresail and upper topsail, and then filled away on the starboard tack. The jib and foretopmast staysail were now set to draw, and the yards had worked around so that the lower topsail would draw on the starboard tack. She was now headed Westerly. If she went Westerly for two days at 2 miles per hour, a total of 96 miles, the net distance covered would be 384 (480 less 96) miles, approximately the distance of 378½ between the probable point of abandonment and the point of actual discovery.

Dr Cobb's explanation for the otherwise strange fact that the abandoned ship had been sailing on her exact course for nearly ten days, while unmanned, seems to fit the facts, and we may conclude that, after she had been abandoned, she continued on her course, holding up into the wind until, some nine days later, a sudden squall, perhaps the one encountered by the *Dei Gratia*, set her about, and she then sailed backwards to the spot where that vessel met her. This natural explanation relieves us of the suspicion that someone was on board.

Several other seemingly suspicious circumstances need to be

disposed of before we can absolve both crews from complicity in foul play. That the derelict's cabin windows were battened up need not alarm us unduly for this was done probably to keep out bad weather and to make the cabin snug. Nor need the marks on the vessel's bows, which Mr Austen thought had been made intentionally, detain us long for the explanation put forward by Captain Shufeldt, that they were caused by splinters forced off by the action of the sea, is quite reasonable. The fact that the cabins and hold were found a foot deep in water can be explained by the likely possibility that the derelict shipped a heavy sea between her abandonment and her discovery. The presence on the ship of the ornamental sword is accounted for by Mr Fay's explanation that it was a memento picked up by Benjamin Briggs on his travels. The smallness of the salvage award, which appears to suggest that Captain Morehouse's claim was viewed with suspicion, can be attributed to the annoyance of the judge when he found that Chief Mate Deveau had been allowed to go out of the Court's jurisdiction.

There remains the 'notice' printed by Mr Keating which reported that Spanish coastguards had found the *Mary Celeste* abandoned on 6 December and that, on the 12th, she was boarded by the men of the *Dei Gratia* who took her away. This alleged incident is employed by Mr Keating to suggest that Captain Morehouse's claim was not above board, and the movements of the *Mary Celeste* on the day before she was brought into Gibraltar, as testified to by Deveau and his men, seem slight corroboration for Mr Keating's suspicions. The vessel in his charge, after making Ceuta light at 6.0 a.m. on 11 December, ran 30 to 40 miles up the Spanish coast, Deveau told the court. But his explanation, that the weather prevented him from getting into Gibraltar and he was swept up the coast, is a reasonable one.

The Spanish government's statement may have been a garbled version of reports by coastguards who had seen the *Mary Celeste* off the coast.

The problem of how the people on the *Mary Celeste* left their vessel has been accounted for. Why they did so is a far more complicated question, one which can be met only with theories. There are two salient facts: they abandoned their staunch and sound vessel in an awful hurry and they deserted her not far from land. The log-slate entry records that, on 25 November at 8.0 a.m. the eastern point of the island of Saint Mary lay six miles distant. After that entry there is silence and we can conclude only that something happened that morning to induce Captain Briggs to launch the boat and place in it his family and crew.

What extraordinary occurrence could have induced their precipitant flight? The captain, officers and crew abandon their vessel in sudden panic, leaving their possessions behind them, Benjamin Briggs having time only to pick up the ship's papers. A vast amount of speculation has been directed to explain what might have caused this hurried flight from a vessel which Mate Deveau described as 'far safer than an open boat'. Both he and Captain Morehouse, as well as Captain Winchester, were invited by the judge to give their opinion as to the cause of abandonment.

In his evidence Deveau advanced the theory that 'there was a panic from the belief that the vessel had more water in her than she had, as afterwards proved'. He thought that the crew, having sounded the pumps, panicked, and thinking the vessel would go down, abandoned her, a theory he thought was corroborated by his discovery of the sounding rod lying by the pumps. Captain Winchester stated his opinion that the captain and officers would not have abandoned their ship from stress of weather only. They would not have deserted her unless in fear of their lives, he declared, for they were men who, in his opinion, would have remained on their ship until the last. Captain Morehouse, according to Mr Lockhart, who corresponded with his widow, always believed that on the morning of 25 November the *Mary Celeste* was becalmed a few miles to the north of the rugged and precipitous coast of the island of Saint Mary; that a current began to drive her towards the shore; and that the crew, in a sudden panic, took to the boat. Probably they intended to stand by and, if a breeze sprang up, to rejoin the ship; but unfortunately they did not take the precaution of attaching the boat by a line to the *Mary Celeste*. So, when the desired breeze came, the brigantine careered away from them and, row as strongly as they could, they were unable to overhaul her. Captain Morehouse believed that ultimately the boat was driven ashore and beaten to pieces at the foot of the cliffs, while all those in her perished.

Captain Winchester advanced his theory as early as 1886 to

Captain Coffin who reported it on 24 January, quoting Captain Winchester as saying:

> The cause of the hurried stoppage of the vessel, of the launching of the boat and of the abandonment was, in my opinion, that the alcohol which formed her cargo being in these red-oak barrels, a wood which is extremely porous, enough of its fumes exhaled through the pores of the wood to mingle with the foul air of the hold and generate an explosive gas which blew off the fore-hatch.
>
> Believing that she was on fire below, and considering the inflammable nature of her cargo, and mindful of the fact that his wife and child were on board, Capt. Briggs, on the spur of the moment, resolved to heave the vessel to, launch the long boat, get into it and remain at a safe distance from the brig awaiting further developments. This was probably done, but the brig's mainsail being stowed, she had no after-sail to keep her to the wind, and she got stern way and backed off until the wind filled her topsail, when, like a frightened deer, away she went, leaving her crew behind. She would run, of course, a couple of miles before she would come to again, and before the crew could row the heavily loaded long boat up to her she would go off again, and so the tantalising chase would be kept up until darkness came on, and then they would lose her altogether.
>
> Of course this is mere theory. Nothing was ever heard of the missing crew, and they were doubtless all drowned, but there is much in support of this theory. In the first place the hatch was found bottom upward, proving conclusively, to my mind, that it had not been taken off by a sailor, for there is a superstition among seamen that if you turn a hatch bottom upward your ship will turn bottom upward before the voyage is ended. The hatchway was forward of the foremast, and led down into the fore-peak, where her stores were stowed, and so it had been customary to go down there frequently, and the hatch had been left unbarred, and not battened down nor caulked, and, therefore, when this explosion took place it just threw the hatch off, and landed it bottom upward on the deck.
>
> I have still further proof in support of this theory. An old captain whom I met in New Haven said to me: 'In such a year I was on the bark so and so, bound to Genoa, from New Orleans, with a cargo of alcohol. One day, sailing along with moderate fine weather, all at once there was an explosion in the main hatch. It burst the tarpaulin, upset the hatch and broke it all to pieces. I saw steam and what seemed like smoke,

coming up through the hatchway, and of course we came to the conclusion that the ship was on fire, and we hove to, lowered the boat, and all hands got into it, except me. As I was about getting into the boat I looked at the hatch and saw that the smoke had ceased to come out. I took a turn with the painter, went to the hatch, found no signs of fire, called the men out of the boat, hoisted her up, filled away, and proceeded, discharging my cargo all right in Genoa in due time.' This was entirely convincing to my mind, and the abandonment of the vessel is no longer a mystery.

Captain Winchester's theory was repeated in 1913, in the December issue of the *Nautical Gazette*, an American publication, by his grandson, Mr Winchester Noyes who, like his grandfather, stated incorrectly that the hatch cover was found upside down on the deck. The salient fact of Captain Winchester's theory is that the cargo actually exploded, of which, we recall, no evidence was found at Gibraltar. Appreciating this fact, Dr Oliver Cobb explained the theory more realistically in *Yachting Monthly*, a British periodical, in August 1925, in an article which was printed also in the American magazine *Outlook* on 1 September, 1926. He wrote:

Now what happened?

This seems to me to be the best theory: A cargo of alcohol sometimes explodes, and it usually rumbles before exploding. It may well be that after the breakfast had been cleared away in the cabin on the morning following the day of the last entry in the log-book, when the vessel would have been about one hundred miles from St Mary's Island, the temperature rising, the cargo began to rumble. The captain would naturally have had the boat lowered and brought quickly alongside, and would have put his wife and child into the boat at once as a measure of safety. After getting the boat alongside, apparently the work of taking in sail was commenced. Someone lowered the topgallant yard, and someone the gaff topsail. At this point I think there was an explosion of gas which blew the fore hatch in the air, and it fell on deck up-side down. Expecting immediate destruction of the vessel, everybody jumped into the boat and shoved off as quickly as possible. They were intent upon one thing only – to reach a safe distance before the great explosion which they momentarily expected. In their haste they neglected to attach a line to the vessel by which they could have been towed, and to take provisions, water, and instruments of navigation.

The cargo did not explode, and the vessel sailed away from them, leaving eleven persons in a small boat a hundred miles from land without compass, food, or water. They perished, how we shall never know.

Dr Cobb, it is necessary to point out, is wrong in two particulars. The hatch cover was found on deck but there is no evidence that it was 'up-side down', and there were only 10 persons on board. To this theory may be added the suggestion made to me by a very experienced deep-sea yachtsman who hazarded the opinion that, when they inspected the cargo, one of the seamen may have been carrying a lamp which ignited the fumes, causing an explosion.

Mr Charles Edey Fay, who had the advantage of discussing this theory with Dr Cobb after he had acquired in 1930 a typed copy of the testimony given at Gibraltar, and written a further article in *Yachting* (a different publication from *Yachting Monthly*) in February, 1940, has attempted to reconstruct the events on board the *Mary Celeste* on 24 and 25 November, 1872. Let us follow his reasoning.

Sunday, 24 November, 1872.

It is noon, and according to the observation taken at this time and noted on the vessel's log, the *Mary Celeste* is in latitude 36 56′ N, and longitude 27 20′ W. All of the Azores group are now astern except San Miguel (St Michael's) off to the northeast about 100 miles distant, and Santa Maria (St Mary's) about 110 miles directly east and therefore practically dead-ahead of the *Mary Celeste*. She is making 8 knots, at which rate she continues until 7 p.m. when, with freshening wind, her speed increases to 9 knots.

The night promises to be a stormy one, and at eight o'clock when the first watch comes on duty, they take in her royal and topgallant sails. By 9 p.m. her speed drops back to 8 knots, at which rate she continues up to midnight. At this time – twelve o'clock midnight – the log reads: 'Knots, 8: Course E. by S.: Wind, west: M.P. rainy.' It is probable that, by this time, at the speed the vessel has been making since Sunday at noon, she has travelled about ninety miles, and must be nearing the western end of Santa Maria (St Mary's) Island. It is a matter of official record that 'stormy conditions prevailed over the Azores on November 24 and November 25.' [Mr Fay prints a letter dated May 27, 1940, which he received from Servico Meteorologico dos Acores.]

Monday, 25 November, 1872.

Midnight is passed and a new and eventful day is beginning. The progress of the vessel continues steadily. One o'clock, two o'clock, three o'clock, four o'clock, the entry against each hour reads the same – 8 knots. Soon the first streaks of dawn will be visible, and now there is land ahead, for the log-slate entry reads: 'At 5, made the island of S. Mary's bearing ESE' and a similar entry appears against the sixth hour. With this bearing it seems that the point of land observed by the vessel's watch must be Ponta Cabrastente which is the *northwestern* extremity of Saint Mary's. The vessel is now, approximately in latitude 37 0′ which is slightly further *north* than her position on the previous day at noon, when she was in latitude 36 56′.

But why, we inquire, is Captain Briggs, or whoever is directing the vessel's course, taking her to the *north* of St Mary's, when it must be known by all hands that, in order to reach Genoa, they must pass through the Strait of Gibraltar, which lies off to the *southeast* in the lower latitude of 35 57′? Surely, he is not planning to land along the island's north shore, as it is well known to all navigators that neither here nor elsewhere on this island are there any harbors where vessels can find safe accommodation. Moreover he must also know, that about twenty-one miles to the northeast of the island's northeast extremity, lies the dangerous Dollabarat Shoal on which the sea breaks with great violence in stormy weather, but whose barely hidden rocks are not visible when the sea is calm. His present course, if continued, will take him between this shoal and the northeast end of the island. With a shifting wind – not an unusual occurrence in these waters – the vessel's position might become a very perilous one – but Captain Briggs is a capable mariner, and it is safe to assume that he will not do anything reckless or careless, especially at such a time when the safety of his wife and child, in addition to that of his crew, is at stake. Can it be that he is ill or otherwise incapacitated, that some accident, or even something more serious, has befallen him, that other hands are directing the course of the *Mary Celeste*? Why is the vessel going into a more northerly latitude, when she should be going to the southward?

[Mr Fay inserts a note here which reads:]

Lieutenant-Colonel J. Agostinho, Director of the Servico

> Meteorologico dos Acores, writing from Angra do Heroismo, Azores, under the date of 17 October 1941, states that Captain Briggs probably feared 'to fall to the South within the limits of the trade winds (blowing from N.E.) which would put the vessel far from her route to Gibraltar'. 'Do not forget' continues the writer, 'that Columbus followed that course when he returned from his discovery, and every sailing vessel coming from Africa or South America to Europe takes the same course.'

Mr Fay continues:

> But now the ship's bell sounds eight times, indicating that it is eight o'clock on this memorable Monday morning. By this time, the vessel, according to the track noted on her chart, has skirted the island's *north* shore, and now comes the final record when the log slate reads: 'At 8, Eastern point bore SSW. 6 miles distant'. After this, silence! A silence which, after the passing of seventy years, still remains unbroken!

This 'Eastern point' was, suggests Mr Fay, in all probability Ponta Castello, at the south east of the island which stands out more prominently than Ponta Matos, at the island's north-east extremity. He continues his reconstruction:

> *Possible Time of Abandonment*
> It seems probable, therefore, that on this Monday, 25 November, at some time after 8 a.m. something of disturbing character happened. Whatever it may have been, it must have been sufficiently serious to cause an experienced master-mariner with his wife, child and crew, to abandon ship, and to do so in haste. As previously mentioned, Deveau testified that 'the men's clothing was left behind; their oilskins, boots, and even their pipes as if they had left in a great hurry or haste.' It is impossible to fix the hour when abandonment took place, but from the condition of the cabin-table on which there was no food; from the appearance of the galley where the stove was knocked out of place and no cooked food was found: from the Captain's bed which was as it had been left, after being slept in, not made – in the menage of Mrs Briggs, beds were not likely to go unmade until afternoon; with no sign of an interrupted or finished meal; no evidence of preparations for serving a meal; no log or log-slate record after 8 a.m. on a vessel where both the log and working chart had been systematically kept up to noon, 24 November; from all of

these considerations it seems reasonable to suppose, and it is our belief that abandonment took place between 8 a.m. and the noon hour on Monday, 25 November.

Possible Cause of Abandonment

It will be recalled that the seventeen hundred barrels of alcohol had been loaded in late October, loading having been completed on 2 November. The *Dei Gratia* following eight days behind the *Mary Celeste*, had experienced stormy weather from the date of sailing 15 November, up to 24 November. During this time her crew never took off their fore hatch, and the main hatch was off for one hour. It is, therefore, probable that the *Mary Celeste* also had encountered stormy weather and that in all likelihood her hatches had remained closed during most, if not all, of the voyage up to the day of abandonment. Under such circumstances, the hold had been getting little or no ventilation. The vessel having left the comparatively cool temperature prevailing in New York at that season, and having passed through the Gulf Stream into the milder climatic areas of the Azores, it would not be surprising if the atmospheric changes had been producing some effect upon a non-ventilated hold containing seventeen hundred barrels of alcohol, some of which may have leaked.

[Mr Fay reminds us that at Genoa, though the cargo came out in excellent condition, nine barrels were found to be empty.]

According to a letter from the Servico Meteorologico dos Acores, 'calm or light wind prevailed on the forenoon of the 25th'. It is possible that Captain Briggs, mindful of the character of the cargo and the necessity for ventilating the vessel's hold, took advantage of the comparatively calm weather and sometime during the forenoon, ordered the removal of the bar of the forward hatch. It was perhaps at this particular juncture that something of unusual character happened. The uprush of fumes from an unventilated hold, into which the contents of all or part of eight barrels of alcohol had leaked, may have been so strong as to alarm the crew, and if it was accompanied by a rumbling or roaring noise, it would have been sufficient to convince all hands that the ship was about to blow up and that their safety lay in immediate abandonment of the vessel.

It appears from the testimony, that the salvors found the fore hatch lying on deck, on the port side of the hatch-way, about three feet away from it. Although there have been newspaper and other reports to the effect that this hatch was found up-side down (which, to a sailor, would indeed have seemed an ominous circumstance, something likely to be remembered and worthy of mention) there is nothing in the testimony to confirm the report. Not a few writers have advanced the theory that an explosion of some kind occurred in the vessel's hold and that the hatch was blown off, but the *Dei Gratia's* men, as well as John Austin, the Surveyor of Shipping at Gibraltar, testified that there were no signs of an explosion. With seventeen hundred barrels, stowed in three or four tiers in the vessel's hold, it would have been difficult, if not impossible, to make a thorough examination at this time. It is, however, a matter of official record, that while the *Mary Celeste* was at Gibraltar, the Marshal of the Vice-Admiralty Court had fifty casks taken on deck from the hold of the vessel.

'The cargo and the stowage', it is reported, 'were found in excellent order, and the casks showed no signs of having been handled in any way, also the contents, the casks being full and in good shipping order.' In the circumstances, the possibility of the occurrence of an explosion of major proportions seems considerably diminished, although it is still a question whether even the removal of fifty casks would have enabled the investigators to see more than a comparatively small part of the remainder of the cargo.

Opinions differ widely as to whether or not leakage from the alcohol would have produced gases, and whether, even if gases were produced, it would have been possible to cause a minor explosion or rumbling sounds in the hold. It is conceivable that the cargo gave forth a noticeable odor. Even apart from the possibility of an explosion, if, on removing the hatch, any vapor accompanied by a strong odor had issued from the hold, there can be no question as to the alarming effect it would have had upon the ship's company.

Mr Fay here quotes Dr Cobb to say that while assisting the mate of the brigantine the *Julia A.Hallock* of which Oliver Briggs was master, in unloading 1,600 barrels of petroleum at Naples, they found the metal hoops of the barrels had become chafed, the sort of friction which could have caused an explosion. Mr Fay does not explain when this took place for the *Julia A.Hallock* was lost in 1872 when Dr Cobb was fourteen years of age. He continues his reconstruction:

Precisely what happened will probably remain for all time in the category of conjecture. According to the theory of Dr Cobb, as we understand it, Captain Briggs, confronted by a sudden and imminent peril, and fearing for the safety of his wife and child, and the members of his crew, gave orders to launch the ship's boat which was lying across the main hatch. As the wind was, presumably, from the west at the time, and the vessel's course was approximately east by south, it is probable that the boat was launched from the leeward side, which, under the circumstances, would then have been the port side of the vessel. As an additional precautionary measure, Captain Briggs may have directed one of his men to break out a coil of rope for a tow-line, so that if the threatened danger should pass they could return to their vessel. The place where such ropes were customarily stowed was the lazarette, a low, head-room space below the deck in the after part of the vessel. According to Dr Cobb's theory, they had already removed the lazarette hatch (reported as found 'off' by the salvors) when it may suddenly have occurred to one of the company that it would take less time to utilize the main peak halyard, conveniently at hand, than to bother with breaking out a new, and perhaps stiff, coil of rope from the lazarette. This halyard, a stout rope of about three inches in circumference, and approximately three hundred feet long, stood ready for almost instant use. According to the Court testimony, the mainsail was furled. The gaff (a spar) of this sail would, therefore, have been resting on it, presumably with a stop around the gaff, the sail and the boom, encircling all three. Assuming that on this vessel the halyard was secured at one end to the gaff (although on some vessels it began at a ring-bolt on the mast-head) and that it ran thence upward and downward, through a treble block on the mast-head and two single blocks on the gaff, it would finally descend to the deck where it would be secured to a belaying pin in the pin-rack or to the pin-rail at the foot of the mast.

According to Dr Cobb's theory it would have taken but a few minutes to release this end of the halyard and then pull it through the gaff and mast-head blocks until its entire length, with one end still secured to the gaff, would have been available for towing purposes. The free end of the halyard could then have been passed between the wooden stanchions (upright struts) supporting the topgallant rail (the vessel having no bulwarks) and then connected with the painter (rope) of the small boat which, by this time, no doubt, would have been alongside, with most of the ship's company already aboard. The tenseness of the situation can easily be imagined as they anxiously awaited the moment when all hands would be in the boat and they could cast off from the *Mary Celeste* and put as much distance as possible between themselves and the danger threatening them. At the end of such a long tow-line, they would doubtless have felt comparatively safe while awaiting further developments. As reported by the Servico Meteorologico dos Acores 'calm or light winds' prevailed on the forenoon of that day, and it seems probable that the abandonment of the vessel occurred during this period of calm, as the launching of a small boat on a wild sea would have meant little more than the substitution of a new peril for the one immediately impending.

The picture thus presented is that of a small boat – probably 16 to 20 feet long with perhaps not more than 9 to 12 inches free-board, carrying ten persons – and a few hastily gathered necessaries, including, no doubt, a small supply of food and drinking water. They are trailing astern of the *Mary Celeste*, somewhat off to port. The vessel's speed which at 8.0 a.m. that morning was recorded as eight knots, must now be considerably reduced, as her mainsail, gaff-topsail, middle staysail, topmast-staysail, topgallant-sail, royal and flying-jib are all furled. Her main staysail is probably lying loose on top of the forward-house as if it had been hurriedly let down, and the only sails set are her foresail, upper and lower topsails, jib and fore-topmast staysail.

If this brief portrayal of the situation conforms at all closely to the actuality, it is reasonable to suppose that the occupants of the boat continued to hope for the eventual return to their vessel. They could not foresee that such hopes were not destined to be fulfilled and that the morning calm was not to continue. Sudden and violent squalls are of frequent occurrence in the Azores, and according to the meteorological report, something of this character must soon have happened for it states that in the afternoon of that date, a wind of gale force prevailed over this area of the Azores. Under the impact of a wind of such violence the vessel may have lunged forward with such suddenness as to break the improvised tow-line, leaving the occupants of the boat striving with frantic but futile effort to overtake the on-sweeping *Mary Celeste*. A heavy rain accompanying such a gale, would have materially increased the difficulties of the people in the small boat, and it is possible that rain was present as, according to the report previously mentioned, at Ponta Delgada, only fifty miles distant, there was a rainfall of 29 mm. between noon on 24 November and noon on 25 November. This, according to the Hydrographic Office at Washington, D.C., meant a precipitation of 1.14 inches, representing a departure from normal, as during the rainiest season, December, the monthly average total is 4.42 inches.

> It is barely possible that the boat, while being towed through rough waters, with her nose held down by a taut tow-line, was swamped by the heavy seas, resulting in the drowning of all on board. Had this occurred, however, it seems probable that some remnant either of the boat or her painter would have been noticed by the men of the *Dei Gratia* when they discovered the *Mary Celeste*. According to Dr Cobb's theory, the tow-line parted at the point where it came over the side of the vessel around the corner of a stanchion.
>
> Presumably, the nearest land was Santa Maria, the eastern point of which, at eight o'clock that morning, bore six miles SSW. This island, the easternmost of the Azores group, with its abrupt and precipitous coast would have offered little accommodation even for a small boat of this character, had wind and wave borne them in that direction, but as it appears from the meteorological report that, after the passing of a 'cold front' between 3 and 8 p.m. on 25 November, the wind veered from SW to NW, it seems more probable that the boat, with its little company, was blown to the southeastward, away from the island and out into the broad reaches of the Atlantic – with about eight hundred miles between them and the coast of Portugal, the nearest land to the eastward, and that they were soon overwhelmed in a gale-swept sea.

The *Mary Celeste*, suggests Mr Fay, 'undirected by human hands, apparently kept her eastward course, however unsteadily, for several days, constituting a menace to every vessel which may have crossed her path, and becoming the plaything of the winds which tore two of her sails and made havoc with some of her rigging.'

Dr Cobb's theory, and Mr Fay's reconstruction of events, may not be entirely satisfactory, but at least it fits the known facts. In their testimony second-mate Wright said, 'I observed no remains of any tow-line', Deveau, 'I saw no remains or pieces of a painter or boat's rope fastened to the rail', and, 'the main peak halyards were broken', seaman Anderson 'there were ropes hanging over the side' and 'there were all kinds of running gear hanging overside – sheets and braces hanging over both sides', and seaman Lund 'the peak halyards were broken and gone'.

Mr Cobb's theory requires the acceptance of three suppositions:

(1) That the cargo of alcohol could have given off fumes which might have caused fear of an explosion which Captain Briggs

believed might blow up the vessel, (2) that, in fear of this happening, the captain, officers and crew all got into the boat and rowed away, and (3) that inadequate precautions were taken to secure the boat to the ship.

The third proposition is the easiest to accept for, as Dr Cobb has suggested, the improvised tow-line may have snapped.

It is highly dangerous to base a hypothesis upon a hypothesis, and it appears almost inconceivable that a ship's captain, especially a man of Benjamin Briggs's experience, would have deserted his ship from fear alone, but we need to recall that the two 'fathers' of this theory, Captain Winchester and Dr Cobb, knew him well and they must have taken their knowledge of him in to consideration in advancing it. Neither seems to have been in doubt that Captain Briggs would have deserted his ship for such a cause, real or imaginary. Benjamin Briggs, if this theory is the true solution of the mystery, was frightened by a shadow; for the investigators at Gibraltar found no evidence of an explosion or fire. But what other explanation fits the facts so nicely? There seems no better alternative, for all the famous solutions were based on the false assumption that the *Mary Celeste's* boats were intact and hanging from their davits. Unlike their advocates, we cannot fall back on an octopus, a homicidal maniac, pirates, plagues, Great Pyramids or Flying Saucers.

The basic mystery about the abandoned derelict has always been – How did her people leave her and what happened to them? That is now no longer a mystery. Why they suddenly abandoned their ship is a question which will always remain to exercise our imagination. It can now be discussed with full knowledge of the facts.

The famous 'credo', the ship under full sail, the long stern chase, the half-eaten breakfast, the ghostly cat, the brightly burning fire, the boats hanging from their davits or secured to their chocks by a skin of paint, are fictions which, like those of other great myths, dissolve under the microscope. Mr Solly Flood started it; he sowed the seed of suspicion. Conan Doyle fertilized the seed; his statement that the boats were intact made the mystery soluble only by extravagant theories. Vivid imagination, not exclusive to Mr Solly Flood, did the rest; no one bothered to check the facts. Now the *Mary Celeste's* yards are stripped almost bare; the half-eaten egg, the plate of steaming porridge, and the peacefully sleeping pussy have dissolved into thin air. So we destroy our gods. But, in mourning their passing, let us spare a thought for the poor people of the *Mary Celeste* at the awful moment of realisation, when they saw their staunch ship draw away leaving them tossing on the open sea. When they knew they were alone, their fears unfounded.

APPENDIX I

Dr Patron's Analysis

Dr J.Patron's Report is dated 30 January, 1873. As this report remained secret for so many years, being suppressed by Mr Flood apparently because it failed to support his ingenious theory of foul play, it deserves to be quoted in full. Dr Patron states:

Gibraltar, 30th January, 1873.

At the request of Her Majesty's Attorney General I proceeded on board of the American brig *Mary Celeste* anchored in this Bay for the purpose of ascertaining whether any marks or stains of blood could be discovered on or in her hulk.

After a careful and minute inspection of the deck of the said vessel some red brown spots about a millimetre thick and half an inch in diameter with a dull aspect were found on deck in the forepart of the vessel, these spots were separated with a chissel and carefully wrapped in paper No. 1.

Some other similar spots were equally gathered in different parts of the deck and wrapped in papers numbered, 2, 3, and 4. Paper No. 5 contained a powder grated from a suspicious mark seen on the top-gallant rail part of which was obtained on board and part from a piece of timber belonging to the said vessel in Her Majesty's Attorney General chambers.

I carefully examined the cabin both with natural and artificial light; the floor, the sides of the berths, mattresses, etc. were searched and nothing worth calling attention was seen that could have any relation with the object of my enquiries.

On the 31 January at 2 o'clock I received from the hands of Mr Vecchio Marshal of the Supreme Court the five papers above mentioned and numbered 1, 2, 3, 4, and 5, and a sword with its sheath found on board the said vessel.

The spots which were in paper No. 1, 2, and 3, were cut in small pieces of about a quarter of an inch long and broad passed through a white thread and suspended half an inch from the bottom of tubes containing a small quantity of distilled water.

The contents of paper No. 4 were put in a small filtering bag as their minuteness would not allow any other process of maceration and the same was done with the contents of paper No. 5.

The maceration went on in the five tubes for two hours and a quarter; the distilled water remaining after this period as clear and bright as in the very beginning of the experiment.

Notwithstanding I left the things as they were till the next day and 23 hours maceration did not produce any alteration in the transparency of the liquid, the water being then heated with the spirit lamp as no precipitate or cloudy aspect appeared, I consider the experiment over and of a negative character.

The stains on the pieces of timber remained unaltered in their aspect and the finger which was passed over them was not tinged or stained in any degree their aspect remaining as it was before maceration.

The contents of paper No. 5 macerated in the bag were then examined with a microscope and nothing particular was seen but a few particles of rust (Carbonate of Iron) and some fragments of vegetable substance (Fibres of Wood).

The sword presented on its blade about the middle and final part some stains of a more suspicious character; although few very small and superficial, their aspect was reddish and in some parts brilliant like albuminous coloured substance, my first impression was that they were really blood stains, examined with an eight or ten diameter magnifying glass these stains presented an irregular and granulated surface; the granules becoming smaller in proportion of their distance from the central and thickest part.

After an hour and three quarters maceration the transparency of the liquid remained unchanged; heat produced no cloudy alteration in it and the result was as negative as in those of the stains found on the deck.

The largest of these reddish spots was carefully grated from the blade and put under a microscope of Doctor Hartnack objective No. 7 and ocular No. 3 corresponding to a magnifying power of 330 diameter. A yellow and imperfectly crystalised substance resembling Citrate of Iron presenting here and there some red granules was seen with some fragments of vegetable ramified fibres; but no blood globules could be detected. Three other stains were tested with Hydrochloric Acid and after a perceptible effervescence a yellow stain was produced of chloride of Iron; the insufficiency of the liquid could not permit of any other experiment.

The blade heated under the flame of the spirit lamp recovered a natural brilliancy after the removal by heat of the superficial crust the sheath of the sword was clean inside and with no mark of any kind.

From the preceding negative experiments I feel myself authorized to conclude that according to our present scientifical knowledge there is no blood either in the stains observed on the deck of the *Mary Celeste* or on those found on the blade of the sword that I have examined.

(Sig'd) J. PATRON
M.D.

EDWARD J. BAUMGARTNER.
Registrar Vice Adm: Court
Gibraltar, 28 July 1887

APPENDIX II

The Report of the Surveyor of Shipping

In his Report, undated but written in time for Mr Solly Flood to enclose with his Report to the Board of Trade in London, dated 22 January 1873, Mr John Austin states under oath that on 23 December, 1872, he accompanied Mr Thomas Joseph Vecchio, Marshal of the Court, and Mr Solly Flood, on board the vessel arrested and 'supposed to be the *Mary Celeste*' found derelict on the high seas and 'carefully and minutely surveyed and examined the state and condition of the said vessel and was occupied therein for a period of five hours'.

2. On approaching the Vessel I found on the bow between two and three feet above the water line on the port side a long narrow strip of the edge of one of her outer planks under the cat-head cut away to the depth of about three eighths of an inch or about one inch and a quarter wide for a length of about 6 or 7 feet. This injury had been sustained very recently and could not have been effected by the weather and was apparently done by a sharp cutting instrument continuously applied thro' the whole length of the injury.

3. I found on the starboard bow but a little further from the stem of the Vessel a precisely similar injury but perhaps an eighth or a tenth of an inch wider wh. in my opinion had been effected at the same time and by the same means and not otherwise.

4. The whole of the Hull – Masts Yards and other Spars were in their proper places and in good condition and exhibited no appearances whatever that the vessel since she had undergone her last repairs or during her last voyage had encountered any seriously heavy weather. Some of her rigging was old but some of her ropes appeared to have been new at the commencement of her last voyage.

5. The peak halyards and throat halyards appeared to be the same with wh. she had been rigged during her last and more than once previous voyage. None of them had been recently spliced and they were all in good working condition. If the peak halyards had been carried away during her last voyage they must have been subsequently spliced wh. was not the case.

6. If the peak halyards had been carried away while the vessel was under sail and the vessel had been abandoned hurriedly and without letting go the throat halyards the gaff would have been carried backwards and

forwards by the wind. The jaws of the gaff would thereby have been destroyed and the mainmast would have been cut into but the jaws of the gaff exhibited no signs of a recent injury and the mainmast was undamaged – in such a case also the Gaff would have ripped the mainsail to pieces.

7. Moreover the main boom would have swayed backward and forward and in the event of there being any strong wind either the sheets would have been carried away or the bolts wld. have been torn out of their deck but they were all uninjured.

8. Upon examining the deck I found the butts and waterways in good condition the pitch in the waterways had nowhere started wh. it must have done extensively if the vessel had encountered seriously bad weather.

9. The Vessel had not bulwarks but was provided with a top gallant rail supported by wooden staunchions the whole of wh. were uninjured nor was there a single stanchion displaced. The water barrels on deck were in their proper places and secured in the ordinary manner but such that if the vessel had ever been thrown on her beam ends or encountered a very serious gale they wld. have gone adrift and carried away some of the stanchions of the top gallant rail.

10. Returning to the bow of the Vessel I removed the forehatch immediately under wh. was a new hawser wh. had never been used and was perfectly dry – Had any quantity of water found its way thro' this hatch the hawser would have exhibited signs of having been wetted. It exhibited none nor did any other of the articles wh. I observed there.

11. I found a forward deck house thirteen feet square and about six feet in height above the deck.

12. The deck house was made of thin planking painted white the seam between it and the deck being filled in with pitch a very violent sea would have swept the deck house away. A sea of less than very great violence would have cracked the pannelling and cracked or started the pitch throughout or at least in some parts of the deck.

13. It had not suffered the slightest injury whatever there was not a crack in the planking nor even in the paint nor in the pitch of the deck seams.

14. The port side of the deck house was divided into two cabins the forward one extended between nine feet six and ten feet across the deck and about six feet nine inches fore and aft the after cabin being on the

same side was about six feet nine inches by six feet nine inches. The forward cabin entered by a sliding wooden door facing the bow of the ship.

15. Close in front of the door of the forward port cabin was a seaman's chest unlocked and at the sides of the door opposite to it was another also unlocked. Both were quite full of seamen's effects of a superior description and mostly quite new. They were perfectly dry and had not had the slightest contact with water.

16. Amongst the articles I observed in one of them was a new cigar case with metal clasp not in the slightest degree rusty. It contained nothing but 3 gold studs set with precious stones and a razor also equally unaffected by water. I also particularly noticed a pair of new instep boots and a pair of new high foul weather boots both perfectly clean a quadrant in its case together with a piece of chamois leather all perfectly dry and uninjured and unaffected by water.

17. I also carefully searched for marks of mildew on all the articles particularly on the boots and the rest of the clothing but could not discover any or any other mark of water wh. I believe I must have discovered if the Vessel had encountered any very bad weather.

18. I then examined the after Cabin on the port side wh. I believe to have been the second Mate's and it contained a seaman's chest similar to those in the forward port Cabin and containing clothes wh. I carefully examined but none of which exhibited the slightest appearance of having been subjected to water.

19. The sills of the doors of these Cabins rise to the height of about a foot above the deck. If water had come into either of them to an extent to have flooded them an inch in depth a great part of the clothing wh. I observed would have shown signs of the water none of wh. were to be seen.

20. The Starboard Side of the Deck house to the extent of about six and a half feet in width aft and about 3¼ feet forward comprised the ship's galley and was entered by a sliding door on the after side.

21. The stove and cooking utensils were in good order and exhibited no appearance of having suffered from exposure to water. Had any quantity of water found its way into the galley it would have immediately passed out thro' a scuttle hole on a level with the deck near the stove or thro' a hole wh. I found in the deck near the hearth into the hold.

22. The forward deck house was lighted by two windows on each side those on the port side were covered by a thin sliding shutter. The after window on the Starboard side was uncovered.

23. None of the shutters or of the windows were injured in the slightest degree. Some of them must have been greatly injured or wholly destroyed if the vessel had experienced very bad weather.

24. On the upper deck of the deck house I found the remains of two sails wh. apparently had been split some time or another in a gale and afterwards cut up as large lengths had been cut off with a knife or other sharp instrument and I subsequently found what I believe to be portions of those sails –

25. On going aft I examined a skylight wh. lights both the main cabin and the Captain's cabin. It consisted of six panes of glass on each side the whole of which had a small piece wanting. Had the ship experienced very bad weather the skylight unless it had been covered which it was not when I surveyed the vessel would have been greatly damaged.

26. The height of the Cabin is increased by means of a false deck raised about 15 inches above the deck of the vessel.

27. The entrance to the Cabin is by means of a companion through a door in the forward side and a sliding hatch.

28. On descending into the main Cabin I found at the foot of the companion an oblong piece of canvas wh. I believe to have formed part of one of the sails which had been split and which I had noticed on the forward house. It had been cut and fitted as a lining for a small recess to which it was carefully fastened with nails or screws and through a small brass hook apparently intended for the purpose of hanging a towel on had been carefully driven into one of the uprights.

29. This piece of canvas had evidently been fixed there before the vessel had sailed on her last voyage. On the port side of the main-cabin was the pantry entered by a door the sill of which was about an inch and a half above the level of the lower deck or floor of the cabin. On the floor of the cabin I found among other things an open box containing moist sugar a bag containing two or three pounds of tea an open barrel containing flour and open box containing dried herrings; also some rice a nutmeg some kidney beans together with several pots of preserved fruits and other provisions in tins covered with paper. The whole of these articles were perfectly dry and had not been in the slightest degree injured or affected by water.

30. On the plate rack was another piece of canvas apparently cut from off the sails which I had observed on the forward house. It was cut into the shape of a towel for which it was apparently used. On the Starboard side of the main cabin was the chief Mate's cabin, on a little bracket in which I found a small phial of oil for a sewing machine in its proper perpendicular position a reel of cotton for such a machine and a thimble. If they had been there in bad weather then they wld. have been thrown down or carried away.

31. The chief Mate's bedding was perfectly dry and had not been wetted or affected by water. Underneath his bed place were the vessel's ensign and her private signal WT. The latter had been altered since it had been used. The letter W having been quite recently sown on.

32. I also found under the mate's bedplace a pair of heavy Seamen's boots for stormy weather greased cleaned and apparently unused and also two drawers containing various articles.

33. In the lower drawer were a quantity of loose pieces of iron and two unbroken panes of glass which wd. have been broken to pieces had the Vessel encountered any seriously bad weather.

34. In the lower drawer were among other things a pair of log sand glasses and a new log reel without any log line.

35. The whole of the furniture and effects in the cabin were perfectly dry and in good condition. None of the articles had been or were injured or affected by water.

36. In the cabin was a clock without hands and fastened upside down by two screws or nails fixed in the woodwork of the partition, apparently some considerable time previously.

37. On entering the Captain's cabin which is abaft the main cabin I observed and examined a large quantity of personal effects.

38. In the centre of the cabin against the partition was a harmonium in very good condition and near to it a quantity of books mostly of a religious kind and which with the exception of a few which I was informed by the Marshal had been removed by him out of the lowest drawer underneath the Captain's bedplace and which were damaged by water were in Excellently good condition.

39. I found also on the floor of the cabin a little child's high chair in

perfectly good condition a medicine chest containing bottles and various medical preparations in good condition.

40. The whole of which articles were uninjured and unaffected by water.

41. The bedding and other effects were perfectly dry they had not been affected by water and were in good condition.

42. I am of opinion that some not large quantity of water had fallen on the floor of the cabin through the sky light and found its way into the bottom drawer under the captain's bedplace.

43. In the cabin I found one of the Vessel's compasses belonging to the binnacle. The card of it had been damaged by water.

44. I also observed in this cabin a Sword in its scabbard which the Marshall informed me he had noticed when he came on board for the purpose of arresting the vessel. It had not been affected by water but on drawing out the blade it appeared to me as if it had been smeared with blood and afterwards wiped. Both the cabins were provided with lamps to be lighted by means of petroleum. They and their glasses were uninjured.

45. On the port side of the Captain's cabin was a water-closet near the door of which opposite to a window imperfectly covered on the outside was hanging a bag which was damp and had evidently been much wetted by rain or spray or both coming in at the window.

46. I was informed by the Marshall that upon his going on board the Vessel for the purpose of arresting her he had found the bag full of clothes mostly belonging to a lady and extremely wet.

47. On the Starboard side of the cabins were three windows two of which intended to light the Captain's cabin were covered with canvas similar to that of which the torn sails were made and apparently cut from it the canvas being secured by pieces of plank nailed into the frame work of the cabin the third window intended to light the chief Mate's Cabin no appearance of having ever been covered and the glass was injured on the side of the Cabin facing the bow of the vessel was another window secured in the same manner and with the same materials as those intended to light the Captain's cabin.

48. On the port side there was a window which lighted the water closet. It was partially covered in the same manner as that last mentioned. There was a port for another window to light the pantry but it had been effectually closed up by a wood made to fit into it.

49. Returning to the deck I found one of the pumps in good order the valve of the other had been removed for the purpose of passing a sounding-apparatus into the well.

50. The sounding apparatus wh. consisted of a metal bolt attached to a line was lying near & was in good order.

51. I then carefully examined the binnacle which I found secured to the deck of the cabin between two battens the original batten on the Starboard Side had been replaced by another roughly made. It was farther secured by cleats on each side.

52. The binnacle was constructed to hold two compasses and a lamp between them with a pane of glass separating the lamp from each compass. Both these panes of glass were cracked perpendicularly and apparently from the heat of the lamp only.

53. One of the compasses was in good working condition and did not appear to have been otherwise during the voyage. The other was missing being the one which I found in the Captain's cabin.

54. The binnacle itself did not appear to have sustained any damage.

55. In my opinion it never could have been carried away by a sea which wd. not have destroyed it & washed it overboard.

56. Such a sea wd. also have swept the decks and carried away the skylight off the cabin the top gallant sail & staunchions and besides doing other damage probably have thrown the Vessel on her beam ends.

57. The whole appearance of the Vessel shows that the Vessel never encountered any such violence.

58 I next examined the after or lazaret hatch which is secured by an iron bar and went into the after hold.

59. I found here barrels of stores and other provisions in good order & condition & in their proper places. The whole of these wd. have been capsized if the Vessel had been thrown on her beam ends or encountered any very violent weather.

60. I also saw there a barrel of Stockholm tar standing in its proper position with the head of the barrel off. none of it appeared to have been

used. Had the Vessel encountered any very heavy weather this barrel wd. have been capsized or at all events some of the tar wd. have been spilt, but not a drop of it had escaped.

61. I found no wine or beer or spirits on board. I made the most careful & minute examination through every part of the Vessel to which I had access to discover whether there had been any explosion on board & whether there had been any fire or any accident calculated to create an alarm of an explosion or of fire & did not discover the slightest trace of there having been any explosion or any fire or of anything calculated to create an alarm of an explosion or of fire.

62. The Vessel was thoroughly sound staunch and strong & not making water to any appreciable extent.

63. I gave directions to Ricardo Portunato an experienced Diver minutely & carefully to examine the whole of the hull and bottom of the said Vessel her stem, keel, Sternpost & rudder while I was engaged on board in surveying her, and he remained under water for that purpose for a time amply sufficient for that purpose.

64. I have now perused and considered the paper writing marked A produced & shown to me at the time of the swearing this my affidavit & which purports to be an affidavit by said Ricardo Portunato in this cause on the 7th day of Jany. now instant.

65. Having carefully weighed & considered the contents thereof & all & singular the matters aforesaid I am wholly unable to discover any reason whatever why the said Vessel should have been abandoned.

APPENDIX III

The Dossier of the *Mary Celeste*

American Record of Shipping

1861	May	*Amazon* launched, Spencer's Yard, Nova Scotia.
	10 June	Registered at Parrsboro, Nova Scotia.
1868	31 December	First Register in name of *Mary Celeste* issued by United States Government to Richard H. Haines.
1869	31 October	Ownership transferred to J.H. Winchester and associates.
1872	5 September	Arrives at New York from Cow Bay, Cape Breton.
	3/22 October	Benjamin Briggs acquires 1/3rd share.
	7 November	Sails for Genoa.
	5 December	Found at sea.
	13 December	Brought into Gibraltar.
1873	10 March	Continues voyage to Genoa.
	19 September	Arrives New York.
1885	3 January	Wrecked on coast of Haiti.

APPENDIX IV

The Documents in the Case

The Transcript of Record, Salvage Claim, 1872–3, Supreme Court, Gibraltar.

Mr. Solly Flood's Report to Board of Trade, *Gibraltar Guardian* 14 February 1873.

The following are in the National Archives, Washington, D.C.:

The correspondence between Consul Sprague and the Department of State, with the German officials and Mr. Solly Flood. The correspondence between the British Minister in Washington and the Secretary of State. The affidavits of John Austin, Surveyor of Shipping and Ricardo Portunato, diver, the Report of Captain Shufeldt, the Analysis of the Supposed Bloodstains by Dr J. Patron, the Inventory of Articles found on the *Mary Celeste*, the Articles of Agreement between Benjamin Briggs and crew, the List of Persons Comprising the Crew, the copy of the Log-Slate 25 November, 1872, and Extracts from the Log of the *Dei Gratia*.

The actual Log of the *Mary Celeste* was returned to the ship's owners and has not apparently survived.

Newspapers, Magazines and Books

1872	*Maritime Register*	11, 18, 25 September 16, 23, 30 October 6, 13, 20, 27 November 18, 25 December	*Mary Celeste* Loading at New York and sailing.
		23, 30 October 6, 13, 20, 27 November	*Dei Gratia* Loading at New York and sailing.
1873		1, 8, 15, 22, 29 January 12, 19 February 19 March 9 April 14 May 4, 11, 18 June	*Mary Celeste* at Gibraltar and Genoa.
		1, 8, 15, 22, 29 January	*Dei Gratia* at Gibraltar and Messina.

Year	Publication	Dates	Subject
1873	*Maritime Register*	12, 19, 26 February 5, 12, 19, 26 March 9, 16, 23 April 7, 14, 21, 28 May 4, 11, 18, 25 June	
1872 –73	*New York Journal of Commerce.*	23 December 11 January 25 February 3, 14 March 9, 21 April 13 May	*Mary Celeste* at Gibraltar and Genoa.
1872 –73	*Lloyds List*	16, 17 December 1, 18, 25 March 17 September	*Mary Celeste* at Gibraltar.
1872	*Liverpool Daily Albion*	16 December	*Mary Celeste* at Gibraltar.
	Liverpool Mercury	16 December	*Mary Celeste* at Gibraltar.
1873	*Gibraltar Chronicle*	31 January	Reports of Surveyor of Shipping and Diver.
	Shipping Gazette	5 February	Reports of Surveyor of Shipping and Diver.
	Liverpool Mercury	February	'Strange Occurrence at Sea'.
	Boston Post	24 February	Suspicions of foul play.
	Gibraltar Guardian	14 February	Report. Flood to Board of Trade.
	New York Journal of Commerce	3 March	Bloodstained sword, etc.
	New York Sun	12 March	Allegations of false register.
	New York Herald	15 March	Winchester's reply.
	Liverpool Mercury	15 March	Captain Shufeldt's Report.
	Nautical Gazette	29 March	Captain Shufeldt's Report.
	Gibraltar Chronicle	24 March	Salvage Award.
	Liverpool Daily Albion	16 May	Rafts.

1884	*Cornhill Magazine*	January	J. Habakuk Jephson's Statement.
	(Reprinted in *Captain of the Polestar*, 1890.)		
1886	*New York World*	24 January	Captain Coffin, 'A Brig Fated to Ill-Luck.'
1887	*Longman's Magazine*	10 August	Clark Russell 'The Mystery of the Ocean Star'.
	(Reprinted in collection of his *Maritime Sketches*, 1888.)		
1894	*McClure's Magazine*	November	Brief account by Robert Barr. *Mary Celeste* sails Baltimore to Lisbon with cargo of clocks.
1902	*Brooklyn Daily Eagle*	9 March	Interview with Mrs. A. G. Richardson, widow of chief mate, who alleges murder committed by crew. Refers to slate entry, 'Fanny my dear wife'.
1904	*Yale Alumni Weekly*	3 March	Address by A. A. Raven (comment on salvage award).
	Chambers Journal	17 September	J. E. Hornibrook 'The Case of the *Marie Celeste*' (Octopus theory).
	New York Evening Post	15 October	Allen Kelley 'Strange Case of the *Mary Celeste*.'
1905	*McClure's Magazine*	May	P. T. McGrath 'Terror of the Sea'. (*Mary Celeste* Sails in 1887!).
	Munsey's Magazine	September	John R. Spears 'Mysteries of the Sea'.
1909	*Gibraltar Chronicle*	?	Letter from Ramon Alvarado of Colombus, Ohio, dated 10 August enclosing cipher message.

1912	*The Digby Weekly Courier* (Nova Scotia)	20 September	Obituary of Oliver Deveau.
1913	*New York World*	9 February	Quotes late Captain James Winchester on theory of alcohol fumes.
	Nautical Magazine	April	'J.S.C.' 'An Unsolved Mystery.'
	Strand Magazine	July	Reprint of article by 'J.S.C.', plus novelists' solutions.
	Maritime Exchange Bulletin	August	Letter from Captain C. B. Parsons dated 9 August, garbled account of conversation with Captain 'Boyce' of *Dei Gratia*, 40 years before.
	Strand Magazine	November	Howard Linford – Abel Fosdyk's Story.
	(Reprinted partly in *New York Times* 23 November.)		
	London *Daily Express*	7 November	R.E. Greenhough 'Skeleton's Tale in a Bottle' (St Paul's Rocks). (Reprinted from *Liverpool Mercury* 1904.)
	(Reprinted by *Washington Post* 19 December.)		
	New York Times	23 November	Comment on Fosdyk story.
1913	*Buffalo Express*	14 December	F.J. Shephard 'The *Mary Celeste*'. Review of mystery and of Fosdyk story.
	Nautical Magazine	December	William F. Bernsten 'The Mystery of the *Mary Celeste*.' Lukhmanoff-Specioti story.
	Nautical Gazette	13 December	K.N. Putman 'The End of the *Mary Celeste*'.
		17 December	'The *Mary Celeste*' Mystery.

1913	*Nautical Gazette*	24 December	Winchester Noyes reviews Fosdyk story and states spontaneous combustion theory.
		31 December	K. N. Putman 'Sequel to *Mary Celeste* Mystery', favours explosion theory.
	New York Times	21 December	K. N. Putman – letter re fumes.
1922	Henry M. Gray *Lloyds Yesterday and Today*		Refers to *Mary Celeste* Mystery.
1924	J. G. Lockhart – *Mysteries of the Sea*		Presents theory which he withdraws in 1927.
	London *Daily Express*	24 September	Lucy – Triggs' story.
	New York Times	12 October	Article by Kathleen Woodward, largely reprinting Triggs' story.
	New York Times	26 October	Dr Oliver W. Cobb, 'A Mystery of the Seas'. Presents fumes from alcohol theory.
1925	*Yachting Monthly* (London)	August	Dr Oliver W. Cobb, 'The Mystery of the *Mary Celeste*', expands fumes theory.
1926	*Chambers Journal*	July	Lee Kay-Pemberton story.
	New York Herald-Tribune	24 July	Editorial comment on Kaye-Pemberton theory, '*The Marie Celeste* Mystery.'
	Boston Sunday Post	8 August	Quotes Mr Arthur Briggs (son of *Mary Celeste's* Master) in refutation of Kaye-Pemberton story.

Year	Source	Date	Remarks
1926	*Boston Sunday Post*	15 August	Quotes Captain Morehouse's widow as to her husband's opinion that gases might have caused fear of explosion.
	Outlook Magazine	September	Dr Oliver W. Cobb 'The Mystery of the *Mary Celeste*' probes weaknesses of Triggs's story.
	Literary Digest	18 September	Resumé of articles on Mystery to date.
	British Journal of Astrology	September	Adam Bushey – 'The *Marie Celeste* Mystery Solved.'
1927	John Gilbert Lockhart		*A Great Mystery of the Sea;* The True Story of the *Mary Celeste.*
1929	Laurence J. Keating		*The Great Mary Celeste Hoax*. Pemberton story.
	London *Evening Standard*	6 May	Interview with Pemberton.
	New York Herald Tribune	29 July	Mrs. Priscilla Richardson Shelton, sister of Mate Richardson, expresses scepticism of Pemberton story.
	New Bedford Standard	4 August	Cooper Gaw, 'Facts Refute *Mary Celeste Solution*'. Denunciation of Pemberton.
	Buffalo News	8 August	Frederick J. Shephard – 'Pemberton is a colossal liar.'
	New York Herald Tribune	11 August	Adverse review of Keating book by Walter Millis.
	New York Times (Book Review)	18 August	Captain David W. Bone calls Pemberton's story 'A Forecastle Classic.'
1929	*New York Times* (Book Review)	1 September	F. J. Shephard challenges D. W. Bone's acceptance of Pemberton's story.

1929	*Saturday Review of Literature*	14 September	Christopher Morley quotes Keating's publisher's blurb, which declared 'the Mystery of the *Mary Celeste* is a Mystery no longer.'
	New York Sunday World	15 September	'William McFee Solves the Mystery of the *Marie Celeste*' i.e. abandoned through fear of explosion.
	New York Times (Book Review)	13 October	Keating replies to his critics. J.G.Lockhart – chapter 'Last Thoughts on the *Mary Celeste*' in '*Strange Tales of the Seven Seas.*' – Exposes Pemberton's story and asks, 'Can it be that Mr. Keating christened his book more appropriately than he intended?'
1930	*Liverpool Echo*	19 March	Reference to advertisement inserted in *Echo* by J. C. Anakin, asking Pemberton to communicate with him. *Post* states Pemberton seen in Liverpool a month ago 'but all attempts to trace him have so far come to nothing'.
	Liverpool Post and Mercury	20 March	
1931	*Quarterly Review*	July	Harold T. Wilkins 'Light on the Mystery of the *Mary Celeste.*' (See also that author's Chapter in his *Mysteries Solved and Unsolved*, 1958).
1933	*Chambers Journal*	March	J.L.Hornibrook 'New Light on the *Marie Celeste*' (pirate theory).

1936			Lt.-Commander R. T. Gould, R.N., Chapter on 'Mystery of *Mary Celeste*' in *Shipping Wonders of the World.*
	Canadian Magazine	May	Burton-Robinson 'Question Mark of the Sea'. Finds no explanation 'quite as satisfying as the statement of John Pemberton' yet 'it is obviously untrue'.
	Boston Globe	26 September	'Why was the *Marie Celeste* Abandoned?' Usual inaccuracies and no solution offered.
1937	*New York Sun*	8 March	By Robert Wilder, repeats inaccuracies.
	London *Daily Herald*	7 May	Captain Arthur Crocker's claim.
	Bangnor Daily News	2 July	Article by Henry Buxton reporting death of Mate Richardson's widow and repeats inaccuracies.
1937	*Bangnor Daily News*	19 October	Further article by Henry Buxton.
	New York Times	1 August	Resume of mystery and theories.
1938	*Readers' Digest*	September	In reprinting excerpts from *Log of Bob Bartlett*, repeats usual inaccuracies and increases number of people on board by 300%.
1939	*Log of the Sea*		Felix Riesenberg 'The *Marie Celeste*' usual inaccuracies plus 'food in galley-pots cooked to crisp'. Quotes Captain Marcus T. Tracy (who was in Gibraltar in 1873) on explosion theory.

1939	*Marine Journal*		Marjorie Dent Candee 'New Light on an Old Sea Mystery', factual errors and refers to 'yellow-fever' theory.
1940	*Yachting* (U.S.A.)	February	Dr Oliver W. Cobb '*The Mystery of the Mary Celeste*' corrects errors and advances abandonment in fear of explosion theory.
	New York Herald Tribune	8 February	'The Truth About an Old Friend', states that Dr Cobb's theory carries conviction, but declares that the *Mary Celeste* like the *Flying Dutchman* 'seems forever proof against shere verisimilitude'.
1940	*Maritime Register*	17 July	Article re-stating several errors.
1942	London *Sunday Dispatch*	19 August	Commander Campbell 'I have Solved the Mystery'. Charles Edey Fay – *Mary Celeste: The Odyssey of an Abandoned Ship.*
1943			Rupert T. Gould – *The Stargazer Talks:* Chapter *on Mary Celeste.*
1954	London *Evening News*	3 August	Article in series 'The World's Strangest Stories by Dudley Pope.
1955	London *Evening News*	30 August	'Snatched into Space' by M. K. Jessup.
1961	London *Sunday Express*	17 September	Article by Edgar Lustgarten.

Index

34